D1017095

Golf Foreplay

Published by Sellers Publishing, Inc.

All interior and back cover photographs are by Steven Dinberg
with the exception of photos on pages 16, 17, 44, 73, 115, 128, 140,
147, 156, 161, and 215, which are by Ken Altshuler and
appear courtesy of The Woodlands Club.
Cover photograph and photograph on page 218 by François Gagné
Art direction and styling for cover photograph by Leslie Evans:
Leslie Evans Design Associates, Inc.
The specialty golf club covers that appear on page 218
are courtesy of Creative Covers for Golf.

Sellers Publishing, Inc.
161 John Roberts Road, South Portland, Maine 04106
Visit our Web site: www.sellerspublishing.com • E-mail: rsp@rsvp.com

ISBN: 13: 978-1-4162-0629-3

Library of Congress Control Number: 2010933895

10 9 8 7 6 5 4 3 2 1

Printed and bound in China.

Golf Foreplay

Everything You Need to Know About the Game – Before You Try to Hit the Sweet Spot

By **Ken Altshuler**

Photography by Steven Dinberg

Contents

Introduction

Welcome to the wonderful world of golf. Prepare to get addicted. I started playing golf in 1997 at the young age of forty-five, and it took me about three minutes to become a confirmed golf addict. Of course, it did take me a while longer to feel comfortable hitting a ball in public, but after reading a ton of golf books and magazines, taking a number of lessons, and even attending two golf schools, I acquired the confidence to approach the first tee with bravado and confidence. I promptly hit my first drive right into a tree; it bounced back behind me and ended up going a negative fifteen yards. But at least it gave me a swell story with which to start this book.

I knew that eventually I would be able to hit a drive with a reasonable chance that it would travel forwards rather than backwards. What I didn't know then that I do know now is that a competent golfer will not mind playing with a beginning golfer. In fact, a seasoned golfer loves to share his passion with a new player. What a competent golfer does mind is playing with any golfer who does not know or observe the rules and etiquette of golf.

If the beginning golfer hits three drives out of bounds and decides to try a fourth, that will disturb a competent golfer (see chapter thirteen). If the beginning golfer is twenty yards directly in front of another golfer and is oblivious to the golfer behind him preparing to hit his ball, that will frustrate a competent golfer (see chapter thirteen). And if the beginning golfer stomps all over the putting line of another golfer, that will irritate a competent golfer (see chapter sixteen).

So this book is not intended to make you a competent golfer. Its aim is to make you savvy about the fundamentals of golf – the rules, etiquette, and social nuances of the game. My goal is to teach you all the things you need to know how to do and all the things you don't realize you're not supposed to do, so that you can feel confident playing with any group of golfers regardless of their proficiency. Or yours.

Does this mean that you should not buy or read this book if you are a seasoned golfer? Of course not! You would be amazed at how many rules and procedures are misunderstood and misapplied on a daily basis. Just take a look at the right way to drop a golf ball off a cart path (see chapter 4) and you will know exactly what I mean. So my goal is to inform and entertain you regardless of your expertise or level of play.

And speaking of entertainment, remember, golf is a game and is supposed to be a fun game at that. Towards that end, I begin every chapter with a golf joke. *Why?* you may ask. Because, first, I love a good joke and, in particular, a good golf joke. More importantly, there are moments when your group will be waiting on the tee while the group in front of you is looking for that lost ball. What's the best way to while away your time and minimize your irritation at not being able to hit away? Tell a joke! So I not only give you eighteen jokes to tell, but I give you advice on how and when to tell them.

So read on and embrace the wonderful world of the greatest game on earth.

A JOKE TO TELL WHEN YOUR PARTNER MISSES THAT ONE-FOOT PUTT.

LARRY WAS NOT ONLY A GOLF FANATIC, BUT ALSO A DEEPLY RELIGIOUS MAN. EVERY SUNDAY HE WOULD GO TO CHURCH IN THE MORNING AND THEN END HIS HOLY DAY WITH A ROUND OF GOLF.

BUT LARRY WAS GETTING OLDER AND, ONE AFTERNOON, AFTER FEELING PARTICULARLY FATIGUED, HE TURNED TO HIS WIFE, LOIS, AND SAID, "I REALLY HOPE THERE IS GOLF IN THE AFTERLIFE."

LOIS, SENSING A SADNESS IN LARRY, SUGGESTED THAT HE GO TO CHURCH AND PRAY ON HIS CONCERNS. SO LARRY HEADED TO CHURCH. AS HE BOWED HIS HEAD, HE SAID, "LORD, I AM SO GRATEFUL FOR EVERYTHING YOU HAVE GIVEN ME. MY HEALTH, MY CHILDREN, MY WIFE AND MY GOLF GAME. I HOPE THAT WHEN I GET TO HEAVEN I CAN STILL PLAY GOLF."

SUDDENLY A BOOMING VOICE CAME FROM ABOVE. "LARRY, THIS IS GOD. I HEAR YOUR PRAYERS AND I WILL ANSWER YOUR QUESTION. WHAT DO YOU WANT FIRST, THE GOOD NEWS OR THE BAD NEWS?"

LARRY THOUGHT ABOUT IT A MINUTE AND SAID, "I GUESS GIVE ME THE GOOD NEWS FIRST."

GOD ANSWERED, "THE GOOD NEWS IS THAT IN HEAVEN WE HAVE THOUSANDS OF INCREDIBLE GOLF COURSES. YOU CAN PLAY ANYTIME YOU WANT, PLAY IS NEVER SLOW, AND YOU WILL NEVER LOSE A GOLF BALL."

LARRY WAS THRILLED. "LORD, THAT'S WONDERFUL NEWS. YOU HAVE ANSWERED MY PRAYERS. BUT WHAT IS THE BAD NEWS?"

GOD REPLIED, "YOU TEE OFF TOMORROW AT 9:00 A.M."

Chapter 1

A Blast from the Past: A Short History of Golf

Everyone who plays golf, at some time or another, will be expected to opine on the origins of golf. While that may sound easy, it can be as controversial as the debate over which college football team is the best in the country (which, by the way, is my alma mater, Michigan).

One easy way to resolve this issue is to determine the national heritage of the majority of the players in your group. If you are playing with Italians, golf started in Rome. If the majority of your group is from Ireland, of course golf originated near the lakes of Killarney. And if you are playing with a Midwesterner from the United States, golf began on the farmlands of Iowa (but let me assure you that golf did not begin in Iowa, or the United States for that matter).

What transcends all national turf wars is the general agreement that golf, as we know it today, began in Scotland. Around the twelfth century, shepherds idled their time away by knocking stones into rabbit holes on the current site of the Royal and Ancient Golf Club of St. Andrews, Scotland. If that isn't enough to solidify Scotland's claim as the birthplace of modern golf, the rules of playing the game were established by the Honorable Company of Edinburgh Golfers in Leith, Scotland, in 1744. The St. Andrews Society adopted these rules and over the next century took over the administration and development of the game. The Royal and Ancient Golf Club of St. Andrews set the rules and standards for the world's golfers until 2004, when it turned the job over to a group of companies known as the R&A. Put simply, the Old Course at St. Andrews is the Holy Grail of golf. If you tell your playing partners that you walked across the bridge on the eighteenth hole of the Old Course you will be revered and envied for all eternity.

Payne Stewart approaches the eighteenth green at the Old Course.

The first golf course in North America? Nope, not in Iowa. Not even in the United States. On November 4, 1873, the Royal Montreal Golf Club was born. It would be eleven years before a similar golf club was established in the United States.

In 1884, a group of Scots, Englishmen, and Americans laid out a nine-hole golf course in White Sulphur Springs, West Virginia. Designed by Russell Montague of Pittsburgh, Pennsylvania, they named the course the Oakhurst Links and its first hole is the oldest golf hole still in play in America. Of course, many historians ignore the Oakhurst Links and credit The St. Andrews Golf Club of Yonkers, New York, formed in 1888, as the first permanent golf club to form in the United States. But where would golf be without a little controversy? Did I say a *little* controversy?

Actually, the very creation of the United States Golf Association (USGA), the current governing body of golf in the United States, arose from controversy and bad sportsmanship. What, bad sportsmanship in golf? Impossible! But true. In 1894, both The St. Andrew's Golf Club, which had moved from Yonkers to Hastings-on-Hudson, New York, and the Newport Country Club in Newport, Rhode Island, evidently without the other club knowing about it, hosted an invitational golf tournament. Each golf club declared that the winner of their tournament would be the "National Amateur American Golf Champion." Charles Blair Macdonald, who eventually gained fame as a course architect, was heavily favored to win both tournaments. However, in the final eighteen holes of the Newport tournament, he shot 100 and lost to one W.G. Lawrence. A month later, Macdonald lost in the finals of the St. Andrew's tournament in a playoff, when he sliced his tee shot into a cornfield (hmm, maybe Iowa is not such a stretch after all). Being a bad loser, Macdonald suggested that neither tournament could determine a national champion and that only an "official" golf tournament could do so. Thus, the birth of the USGA.

Now that you have wowed your playing partners with your vast and detailed knowledge of the origins of golf, do not destroy your credibility by repeating the old wives' tale that the word "golf" stands for "Gentlemen Only, Ladies Forbidden." In actuality, there is no clear agreement as to the origins of the word "golf." Maybe the good citizens of Iowa can lay claim to coining the word. At least no one can prove them wrong.

A JOKE TO TELL WHILE YOU ARE LINING UP YOUR BIRDIE PUTT.

JIM MET JUDY AT A PARTY AND IT WAS LOVE AT FIRST SIGHT. AFTER A WHIRLWIND ROMANCE, JIM PROPOSED TO JUDY. HOWEVER, HE TOLD HER THAT BEFORE SHE GAVE HIM HER ANSWER, HE WANTED TO BE COMPLETELY HONEST WITH HER.

"JUDY, GOLF IS MY FIRST LOVE IN LIFE. I THINK ABOUT GOLF ALL THE TIME. I TRY TO PLAY AT LEAST FIVE TIMES A WEEK. I WILL BE A DEVOTED HUSBAND TO YOU, BUT I WANT TO BE HONEST WITH YOU AND LET YOU KNOW HOW MUCH GOLF MEANS TO ME."

JUDY RESPONDED, "JIM I REALLY APPRECIATE YOUR HONESTY. AND SINCE WE ARE BOTH BEING SO HONEST, I FEEL I HAVE TO TELL YOU SOMETHING ABOUT ME. I'M A HOOKER."

JIM THOUGHT ABOUT IT A MINUTE AND RESPONDED, "YOU KNOW, I THINK IF YOU CHANGED YOUR GRIP YOU COULD STRAIGHTEN THAT OUT."

Chapter 2

Golf Lingo You Must Know

Eventually you will hear all of the following terms in a round of golf. Now you can make sure you know what they mean!

ADDRESS

This is neither where you live nor where the golf course is located. You are addressing the ball when you place your club behind the ball prior to swinging at it.

ALBATROSS

A score of three under par. That would be like getting a hole in one on a par 4. That means driving your ball three to four hundred yards and it goes into the hole. If you can score an albatross you do not need to read this book or any other golf book for the rest of your life. An albatross is more often known as a "double eagle." I will summarize the range of "under and over par" terms under "par" on page 24.

APPROACH SHOT

This is any shot you are taking before you reach the green in the hopes that you will actually reach the green on that shot.

APRON

The grass around the perimeter of the green. Also known as the "fringe."

AWAY

The golfer who is farthest away from the hole. Also, where you want to go after a bad shot.

BANANA BALL

Before I start talking about balls going right or left, a disclaimer: Right and left assumes a right-handed golfer. If you are a left-handed golfer, what is right is left and what is left is right. Right? So a banana ball is a "slice" – that is, the ball curves to the right in the shape of a banana (of course, who says a banana curves to the right? If you flip it over it curves to the left. This is what happens when you use fruits to describe a golf term). Bananas are good for you. Slices are not. The range of shots that go too far to the left or too far to the right will be reviewed under "snap hook" on page 280.

BIRDIE

A score of one under par. Doable. If you hit a duck on the pond because you sliced the ball that is not a birdie. That would be manslaughter. Or duckslaughter.

BITE

Heavy backspin applied to a ball that causes it to stop quickly on the green instead of rolling off. You will hear players yell "bite" when they want the ball to stay on the green. Never works for me.

BOGEY

A score of one over par. More common than a birdie.

BREAK

The way the ball is going to roll on the green. If it is going to "break left," it is going to roll to the left after you putt it. If you think the break is to the left, it is probably to the right. That's called Murphy's Law. By the way, when you say you can't get a break, that's whining and self-pity and has nothing to do with what direction your ball is going to roll. And them are the breaks!

BUMP AND RUN

A bump and run is an alternative to standard wedge play. You are off the green and instead of chipping it high in the air (where a bird can snatch it), you hit it low on the ground (that's the bumping) to run up to the pin and, who knows, maybe right in the cup! Nicely played.

BUNKER

A sand trap is a bunker. Or a bunker is a sand trap. Both are equally evil.

CARRY

A carry is how far you have to hit the ball in the air to reach your desired destination, typically to get over a hazard.

CASUAL WATER

This is water that isn't supposed to be on the course. The course designer didn't put it there; it rained a lot the night before and the water hasn't dissipated. If you see water puddling around your feet when you are standing near your ball, this is casual water. You can drop your ball outside this area, but no closer to the hole, without a penalty. However, let me caution you: Any time you take a drop that the rules allow without penalty, it doesn't hurt to have the other players in your group concur with your decision. It's much better to get them to agree beforehand than to give them something to debate when you win the match by one hole.

CHIP SHOT

A chip shot and a "pitch shot" (see page 24) are both part of your "short game" (see page 27). Both shots are made when you are close to the green, but the grass between you and the flag makes putting impossible. A chip shot rolls more than it flies in the air. A pitch shot flies in the air more than it rolls. But a pitch shot is typically a shot from farther away than a chip shot. Got it? It's all a matter of degrees, although golf is a game of inches.

CHUNK

If you chunk the ball, you have hit the ground before you have hit the ball. It will take a large chunk of dirt out of the ground and the ball won't go very far. Also called a "fat" shot. If you chunk the ball on a chip shot, and it goes a very short distance because of this, you will hear it referred to as a "chili dip" or "chili dipping."

CLOSED STANCE

Okay, follow me on this. Imagine a line on the ground from the ball to the target. If your front foot is closer to that line than your back foot, you have a closed stance. A closed stance should cause a shot to "draw" (see page 18). It never works for me. By the way, this may shock you, but this is the opposite of an open stance. What a surprise!

A golfer with a closed stance promotes a draw.

CONDOR

A score of four under par. I mean, really. Have you ever heard of anyone having a hole in one on a par 5? Driving over five hundred yards? Whoever thought up these terms! By the way, logic dictates that this would be a triple eagle. Still ridiculous. Also a really ugly, almost extinct vulture from the West Coast. Unrelated.

CROSS-HANDED

I am including this term because I use a cross-handed putting grip. The conventional grip is to have the right hand below the left hand. I place my left hand below my right hand. Being oppositional comes easy to me.

CUT

In a golf tournament, the threshold that golfers must score to continue to play in the tournament. For example, if the cut is even par, all players who score above par are eliminated and they get the weekend off (not exactly voluntarily). Those that scored par or better "make the cut" and continue to play for the remainder of the tournament. There is usually one cut during the tournament and it is typically after the second round of a four-round tournament. After all, you can't have a hundred golfers milling around on the last day of a tournament, can you?

CUT SHOT

A cut shot curves from left to right (for right-handed golfers, remember). Also called a fade. You will hear players yell, "Cut, cut" when the ball is going too far to the left of the green. Wishful thinking.

DIVOT

The mark made on the ground when your club hits the ball. If you hit the ball correctly you will probably leave a divot. If you hit the ball incorrectly you will dig a trench instead of a divot. By the way, when the ball hits the green it leaves a "pitch mark," not a divot. Don't ask me the difference. I am still trying to fill in the trench I left with my 5-iron. Which reminds me: If your cart has a seed/sand mixture to pour on divots in the fairway, do so. You can also take the parcel of earth your club deposited ten yards away and replace it on the crater you left behind, although a sand/seed mixture works better if you have both options. And always, always, always fix your pitch marks on the green.

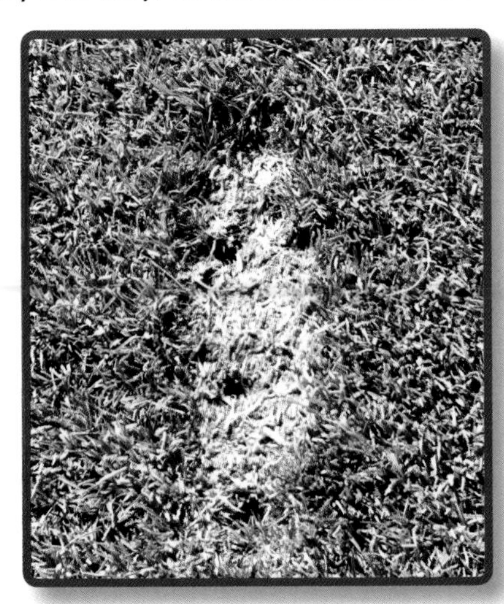

A divot should be filled in with the dug-out sod or a seed/sand mixture.

DOGLEG

When a hole doesn't go straight and bends significantly left or right it is a dogleg. A dogleg left bends to the left. I bet you can figure out what a dogleg right does. Now, how did they come up with this name? Of course! The hole looks like a dog's leg!

DOUBLE BOGEY

A score of two over par. Much more common than an albatross!

DOUBLE EAGLE

A score of three under par. Much better than a double bogey. Also called an albatross, of course. Should rhyme with impossible.

DRAW

A draw is a shot that goes ever so gently to the left (if you are right-handed). A draw does not go so severely to the left as to put you in the rough or woods. Hence, it's a "gentle" curve as opposed to the "duck hook" described below.

DRIVE

It all begins with the drive. The drive is the first stroke played from the tee box on any par-4 or par-5 hole — yes, you do play a first stroke from a par-3 hole, too, but for some unknown reason we don't call it a drive. Maybe that's because you usually use your driver on your first stroke from all par 4s and 5s, but typically not from a par 3 because a par-3 hole is a shorter distance than you can usually hit your drive (hopefully). Of course, you do not have to hit your first stroke from any hole with your driver. You can use any club in your bag, although I wouldn't recommend driving with your putter. Just as I wouldn't recommend putting with your driver.

DUCK HOOK

This is a ball that is hit with so much side spin (not on purpose, of course) that it hooks drastically to the left. It doesn't go very far either. Ugly, ugly shot. This shot "ducks" and your playing partners should, too.

EAGLE

A score of two strokes under par. Not impossible, but still uncommon for amateurs. A hole in one on a par 3 is an eagle.

EXECUTIVE GOLF COURSE

No, this is not a course at which you can play only if you are an officer of IBM. An executive course is a shorter (typically nine-hole) course that is designed to play easier so that the executive can get on and off faster and make it to the board meeting on time.

FADE

This is a shot that curves slightly to the right. Once again, too much to the right becomes a slice. Too much of a slice goes onto the highway.

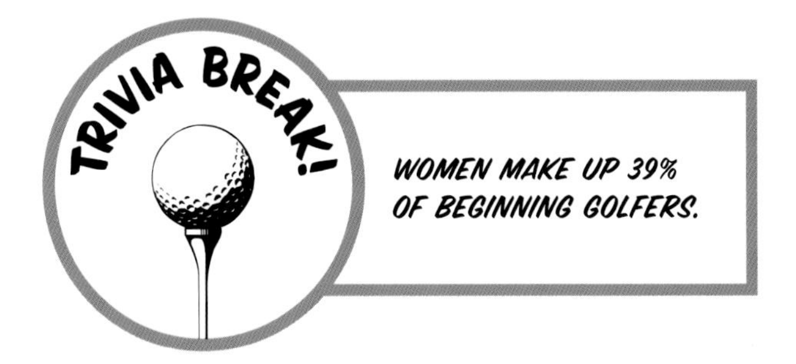

FAIRWAY

The fairway is the closely mowed area of the golf course, between the tee box and the green, where you are supposed to land your ball (rather than in the woods, the water, or the rough). You won't be able to do this every time. Even pros can't land all of their shots on the fairway. But if you do, you get an A+ for effort. And your next shot is much easier from the fairway than anywhere else you may (unfortunately) land.

FIRST CUT

It is a great coincidence that this term follows the definition of fairway, because the first cut (or the first cut of rough) is right next to the fairway. It is grass that is grown slightly higher than the grass on the fairway, but not so high that it's impossible to hit out of it. So you have the fairway leading from the tee box to the green and you have the first cut of rough on both sides of the fairway. What is on the other side of the first cut of rough? The "primary rough" (see "Rough," page 26). There is also a first cut of rough and a primary rough around the green, which are identical to the roughs you find next to the fairway.

FLOP SHOT

Not an easy shot to do, although professional golfer Phil Mickelson makes it look simple. The ball is on top of a lot of grass, and it's close to the green. You are on the wrong side of the sand trap (it's directly between you and the hole), there's about five feet of green after the sand trap. You open your club so it is almost parallel to the ground and hit the ball as a regular shot. The ball goes up in the air farther than it goes forward, lands between the sand trap and the hole, and your playing buddies are in awe. Don't hold your breath.

FORE

This is what you holler when you hit a shot that is going anywhere close to any other human being. If you don't yell "fore" when it is heading towards another golfer you may be calling your lawyer in the morning.

GIMMIE

Always thinking of yourself. Gimmie, gimmie, gimmie. This means that you don't have to actually hit your ball in the hole for it to be considered in the hole. This is a putt given to you when the other golfers assume that even *you* can sink that three-inch putt. Most golfers will concede a putt when the ball is "within the leather" of your putter (which means the length of the grip of your club). If you are given a gimmie, take it and run.

GRAIN

The grain of the grass contributes to which way the ball is going to break on the green. Different grass grows in different directions and the greenskeeper can mow the green in a different pattern. Greenskeepers are evil, I tell you, pure evil.

GREEN IN REGULATION (GIR)

You reach the green in regulation when you are on the green two strokes less than par. If it only takes three strokes to reach the green on a par 5, two strokes on a par 4, or you are on the green with your first hit on a par 3, you are on the green in regulation. The end result is that you can make par if you sink the ball after that with no more than two putts (and birdie with one!).

GROUNDING THE CLUB

This is when your club touches the ground behind the ball at address. You are not permitted to ground the club in a bunker or hazard. You can ground your club in a "waste area" (see page 30).

GROOVE

Well, you are in the groove when your game is smokin' and you can't miss a putt. But that's not really what the golf term "groove" means. Grooves are those little lines on the face of your club. They are intended to create spin on your ball. If they do so, as intended, that is groovy. Peace, man.

HACKER

An unskilled golfer. My middle name.

HANDICAP

When you keep track of your scores you will have a number assigned to you based on your golfing ability and that allows your score to be adjusted compared to other golfers against whom you are playing. To give you a sneak peek of what we'll cover later, a handicap number, based on the slope of a course, is subtracted from your gross score and that gives you a net score of par or better half the time. Got it? Me neither. But we both will have it after reading chapter fifteen on handicaps.

HAZARD

Most golfers consider playing their ball from anywhere other than the fairway or green hazardous. And although hazards are defined in greater detail in chapter thirteen, the rules of golf define a hazard as simply any

bunker or water. That's simplistic, but it's all you need to know for now. If your ball is not on the tee box, fairway, or green, it is hazardous to your golf score. Be forewarned.

HOOK

Goes to the left more than a draw, but less than a duck hook; in other words, a draw that turns out to go so far to the left that you end up in the rough or in the woods. It's the opposite of a "slice," which, as you will see on page 27, goes too far to the right.

HOSEL

That's where the clubhead connects to the shaft. If you hit your ball "off the hosel" it is known as a "shank" (see page 27). And that ain't good either!

LAG

If you are on the green, but so far away from the hole that you may as well be over the county line, your goal is to get it close enough to the hole to have a shot at two-putting the hole. So you will lag the putt as close to the hole as you can.

LAY UP

Intending to hit your ball shorter than you normally could or would to avoid it going somewhere that would make you very unhappy. In other words, a hazard is 170 yards away and it would take a shot of 190 yards to carry the hazard, so you lay up 150 yards to be short of the hazard and not lose your ball and get a penalty stroke to boot. Just beware: When you intend to hit a ball short you will miraculously gain Herculean strength and you will hit that 7-iron thirty yards longer than you ever hit

it before and — you got it — the ball will sail into the hazard. So if you are going to lay up, give yourself plenty of space between the ball and the hazard.

LIE

No, this is not the score your partner told you he got when you know damn well he didn't count those two strokes out of the sand trap. The lie is the ground upon which your ball is resting. You have a "good lie" if you are on the fairway or green. You have a "bad lie" if you are in the bunker, hazard, or on the highway next to the golf course. And that's a good time to lie (say it's your partner's ball).

Good luck getting out of this bad lie.

LINE

The path you expect your ball to go after you hit it. Usually, the line describes the path to the hole when you are on the green. And you never want to walk on your playing partner's line to the hole. It will make him or her grumpy.

LINKS

A links course is on the ocean, and it usually has a minimal number of trees and is typically windy. Think of Ireland or Scotland. Those are almost always links courses. And if you hear someone say, "Let's hit the links," that means "Let's go play golf." Your answer to that should be "I'm packed and ready to go!"

LOOSE IMPEDIMENT

This is a small, natural item, which is not fixed, growing, or embedded in the ground. You can move a loose impediment that may be in front of you (particularly on the green if it is between your ball and the flagstick). You won't receive a penalty unless moving the impediment moves your ball (for example, your ball is off the fairway on a broken twig, you try to remove the twig and the ball moves. Penalty!). But you cannot move a loose impediment in a hazard or a sand trap. Teaches you to keep it on the fairway.

MATCH PLAY

No, this is not trying to light your cigar in the wind. Match play is the competition format in which golfers (individuals or teams) compete against each other hole by hole and whoever wins the most holes wins the match, as opposed to "stroke play" (see page 29).

MULLIGAN

A gift. A do-over. A free shot. It's your partner saying you didn't warm up enough before you started playing. So take a free second shot, but we'll count it as your first shot. A mulligan is not allowed by the rules and not allowed in tournaments, but is absolutely part of a friendly game of golf. Usually.

OPEN STANCE

See "closed stance" (page 16). This is the opposite. Your front foot is farther away from the target line than your back foot. Pros use this stance to fade the ball or prevent a hook. I use this stance when I am not paying attention to how I am standing.

PAR

The holy grail of golf. This is the "professional average result" of a hole, the standard score for a hole. Nirvana. Ecstasy. You get the idea.
So here is the range of scores under and over par, from best to worst: condor (triple eagle), albatross (double eagle), eagle, birdie. par, bogey, double bogey, triple bogey, quadruple bogey, and anything over a quadruple bogey is called a "this is not my day, so I will be in the clubhouse drinking Scotch and watching the latest PGA tournament."

PITCH SHOT

As described under "chip shot" (see page 15), this is a shot that is made when your ball is further away from the green than would warrant a little chip, and goes higher in the air and is expected to land closer to the pin and roll less than a chip shot. "Pitch" is also used to describe the tenor of my voice when I hit the ball into the sand trap instead of onto the green.

PIN HIGH

So you are a hundred yards from the pin. You take your wedge and you hit it exactly one hundred yards. But you hit it to the left or right of the green. If you had hit it straight it would be three feet from the pin. You are pin high, but off the green. Nice try.

PLUGGED LIE

This is when a ball hits wet ground so hard (or from a significant height) that it gets partially buried in the ground. No, you do not have to whack at the ball to get it out of its own crater. You may dig the ball out, clean it off, and drop it as near to the spot as you can, but no closer to the pin — all without penalty. This is your reward for playing in wet conditions. Now if the ball gets embedded in a sand trap, it is called a "fried egg" and you are not allowed to pick, clean, and drop it without penalty. Fairway yes, sand trap no.

A plugged lie on the fairway and a "fried egg" in the sand trap.

PUNCH SHOT

This is a shot played with a very low trajectory, usually required when you are behind or under a tree and you have a huge branch hanging down in front of you. If you don't "punch it out" it is going to hit the branch and land behind you. A punch shot is not what happens if you win your match by seven strokes, and then someone from the other team calls you a "sandbagger" (defined below), and fists start flying. But that would never happen in the gentleman's game of golf, now would it?

PUSH

This is a shot that goes severely to the right, but unlike a slice it starts off to the right the minute you hit it instead of starting out straight and then heading to the right. Doesn't change where your shot ends, but good to know the difference, huh? By the way, a push is also when you are playing a match and no one wins a particular hole. That is a push. It's also called "no blood."

Q-SCHOOL

Q-School is the "Qualifying School," which is a qualifying tournament for several professional golf associations so that pros can earn their "tour cards," making them eligible for the following year's tour.

ROUGH

The "primary" rough is next to the "first cut" of rough (see page 19) and is not just rough but tough. The grass is higher and thicker and more apt to "grab" your club as you attempt to hit the ball out of this area. So we have the fairway (or green), the first cut of rough, and then the primary rough. After that, we have forest, trees, highways, and lots of lost balls. So be happy you are in the primary rough. It could be worse.

SANDBAGGER

This is a person you don't want to play golf with, do business with, or date your sister. This is a golfer who lies about his score so that he has a higher handicap than his skills warrant. A sandbagger inflates his handicap with the intention of winning bets during a round of golf, similar to hustling in pool. A sandbagger will say he has a high handicap, strokes are given accordingly, and then you lose fifteen of the eighteen holes in the round to him. Sandbagger. Synonymous with scumbag.

SANDY

If you get a sandy you have gotten a par or better even though you had to hit out of a sand trap. Way to go!

SCRATCH GOLFER

A player whose handicap is zero. I can only dream.

SHANK

As mentioned above, this happens when a golf ball is struck by the hosel of the club. A shanked shot will scoot a short distance, usually to the right, although it could be severely sliced or hooked. Just an all-around terrible shot.

SHOOTING YOUR AGE

This is when a golfer's score for an eighteen-hole round equals his age. So if you are eighty and you shoot an 80 you are shooting your age. I can't wait to turn 110!

SHOOT YOUR TEMPERATURE

This means shooting a 98. At least you are shooting your age if you shoot your temperature at age ninety-eight.

SHORT GAME

The short game is that part of your game that takes place on or near the green. It includes pitching, chipping, and putting — and, I guess, praying, "Please God, if you let me sink this putt I'll never lie about losing a ball again." Remember the old adage: You drive for show and putt for dough!

SLICE

A shot that goes from left to right. It's more than a fade, maybe the same as a push, but it's a shot that fades rather than starting off in that direction. Hard to believe we have all of these terms for shots that range from too much to the left to too much to the right. But we need to be able to say, "What a terrible slice" and to hear the answer, "No, actually, that was a push, not a slice." And then you can get into a long discussion about what the difference is without having to deal with the fact that your shot just went into the woods.

SLOPE RATING

Slope rating is a number, from 55 to 155, set by the USGA, to determine the level of difficulty of a golf course for a bogey golfer. An "average" course has a slope rating of 113. This is part of the calculation of a golfer's individual handicap (defined in chapter fifteen).

SNAP HOOK

Similar to a duck hook, but slightly different. Though it goes way too far to the left, a snap hook is similar to a push, in that the ball starts out going to the left immediately rather than starting out sort of straight and then hooking to the left. Can also be called a "pull hook." But, anyway you slice it, it is a hook. Not a slice. Oh, never mind.

So here is the spectrum of shots for the right-handed golfer, from left to right: snap hook, duck hook, hook, draw, straight (yeah, right), fade, slice, and push.

Now, you'll notice that there's not an equivalent aquatic animal that's assigned a name for a slice or push that goes as far to the right as a snap or duck hook goes to the left. So I am going to invent a new name for such a hit (I have to get my name in golf history somehow). Let's call it a "mallard slice." If Gene Sarazen can invent the sand wedge, I can certainly invent a golf term!

SNOWMAN

A snowman is a score of 8 on any hole. The figure looks like a snowman, so if you got an 8 on any hole you got a snowman. Even in summer.

STROKE PLAY

No, stroke play is not what can happen if your ball is fifty yards in the woods and you keep swinging at it, hoping to get back to the fairway before sunset. In match play, whichever golfer or team gets the most holes on a hole-by-hole basis is the winner, while stroke-play competition compares the total number of strokes for the preset number of holes (either nine or eighteen) and the golfer or team with the fewest strokes wins. I shoot a 95, you shoot a 94, you win, I lose. Simple. Sad, but simple.

SWEET SPOT

The location on the clubface where the optimal ball-striking results are achieved. The closer the ball is struck to the sweet spot the higher the power transfer ratio will be. And that's good. That means you hit it as well as you can and it will go the maximum distance you can hit the club. Sweet, huh?

TAP IN

A ball that has ended up so close to the hole that even your competitor should concede the putt. But, if he doesn't, there's not a chance in the world you will miss the putt because all you have to do is tap it in.

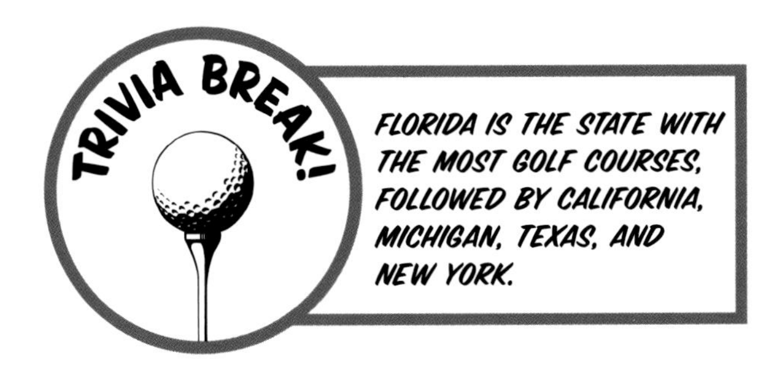

TENDING THE FLAG

This means you are holding the flagstick for another golfer while that golfer is putting. Just remember to take out the flag as the golf ball approaches.

THIN SHOT

If you hit the ball too high — on its top instead of squarely in the middle — you have hit it thin. This is the opposite of hitting it fat. The ball will often go farther than intended when you hit the shot thin, although everyone knows that you did not hit the ball as you intended to hit it.

TOPPED BALL

Good thing this comes right after the definition of a thin shot, because it is almost identical. A topped ball is one that is hit so high that it barely grazes the top, resulting in your shot traveling a very short distance (well under ten yards — not good). A thin shot goes farther than intended and a topped ball will not go far at all.

TURKEY

A turkey is three consecutive birdies during one round of golf. I can only imagine getting a turkey. But if I get three consecutive birdies during one round of golf I will not mind being called a turkey.

UP AND DOWN

If you are off the green and you chip the ball close to the pin and you sink it with one putt you have gotten "up and down" from off the green. Nicely done! Also called "up and in." Good no matter what you call it.

WASTE AREA

A waste area is the twilight zone of a golf course. It is within the boundaries of the golf course, but it's not a sand trap or a hazard, and it's certainly not the fairway or the green. It can be an area of crushed limestone, sandstone, gravel, sand, or just hard dirt. Your ball is in play in a waste area and must be hit where it is, without relief. However, unlike a hazard or sand trap, local rules usually allow you to ground your club before attempting to hit out of a waste area. How do you know you are in a waste area? Well, it's kind of like pornography: Hard to define, but you know it when you see it. Typically, one side of the waste area is not defined, or edged, like a bunker. In any event, being in a waste area will make you want to get wasted by an alcoholic beverage. But don't. It won't help you get out of the waste area.

WHIFF

This is really embarrassing. This is swinging at the ball and missing it completely. You can pretend it was a practice swing, but we all know you were distracted by thoughts of your stock portfolio. And, yes, it counts as a stroke. Bummer.

THE YIPS

Ah, the yips. The yips have actually ended the professional career of many a fine golfer. This is a tendency to twitch during the putting stroke. If you have the yips you are in good company: Sam Snead and Ben Hogan both suffered from the yips during their careers. Not fun. It will require years of psychotherapy to correct.

A JOKE TO TELL WHILE YOU ARE WASHING YOUR GOLF BALL.

A DOCTOR, LAWYER, AND ACCOUNTANT WERE PLAYING BEHIND A PARTICULARLY SLOW GROUP OF GOLFERS. FINALLY, THE RANGER CAME BY AND THE ACCOUNTANT ASKED HIM WHAT WAS UP WITH THE SLOW PLAY.

THE RANGER RESPONDED, "THAT'S A GROUP OF BLIND FIREFIGHTERS. THEY LOST THEIR SIGHT SAVING OUR CLUBHOUSE FROM A FIRE A FEW YEARS AGO, SO WE LET THEM PLAY FOR FREE ANYTIME THEY WANT."

THE DOCTOR RESPONDED, "YOU KNOW THERE IS AN OPHTHALMOLOGIST IN MY OFFICE. I'M GOING TO ASK HIM IF THERE'S ANYTHING HE CAN DO FOR THEM."

THE ACCOUNTANT SAID, "GREAT IDEA. I AM GOING TO OFFER TO DO THEIR TAXES FREE FROM NOW ON."

THE LAWYER CHIMED IN, "CAN'T THEY PLAY AT NIGHT?"

Chapter 3

A Round of Golf Courses and Golf Players

NINE COURSES YOU SHOULD RECOGNIZE

A great way to compensate for being a mediocre player is to know a whole lot about the game itself. Then, if you want to distract other players from your second out of bounds tee shot you can mention how hole number 6 reminds you of that great shot Tiger Woods made in his first British Open on the fourteenth hole of the Old Course at St. Andrews. Keep in mind that the debate over the most important golf courses and golf players in the world is about as controversial as the origins of golf, but these are the courses and players with whom you need to be familiar if you intend to distract your fellow golfers.

1. The Old Course at St. Andrews Links, St. Andrews, Fife, Scotland — Scotland is the Holy Grail of golf and St. Andrews is its most beautiful jewel. First played around 1552 and considered THE course to play if a golfer is to die happy. The Old Course is not only recognized as the most famous and important course in the universe, it is also generally recognized as the template for the now-standard eighteen holes. (Old wives' tale alert: a golf course does not have eighteen holes because there are eighteen shots in a bottle of whiskey.)

2. Pine Valley Golf Club, Pine Valley, New Jersey — Often considered the best golf course in the United States, with the best collection of par 3s and par 5s in the world. Pine Valley is a highly exclusive club, allowing males to join solely by invitation from the board of directors. But don't worry if you never get to play here: So far, even Tiger Woods hasn't played the course. But if you do get to play it, please call me and let me know the secret handshake.

3. Augusta National, Augusta, Georgia — Augusta National plays host to the first "major" golf tournament of the year, the Masters, the only major that is held at the same course every year (since 1934). The course is also well known for its botanical beauty, being lined with beautiful azaleas and trees that are more than one hundred years old. The Masters is also famous for awarding the annual champion a green sports coat with the club's logo on the left breast. However, the green jacket has to be returned when the next Masters is held the following year because only the current winner can possess the green jacket.

4. Pebble Beach Golf Links, Pebble Beach, California — This is widely regarded as one of the most beautiful courses in the world, hugging the rugged California coastline with wide-open views of the ocean. However, it's not an easy course to play. When the 2000 U.S. Open was held at Pebble Beach only one player finished under par: Tiger Woods set a U.S. Open record by finishing 12 under par. His score was a full fifteen shots better than the runners-up and the largest margin of victory ever recorded in a major championship.

5. Pinehurst #2, Pinehurst, North Carolina — Pinehurst #2 is considered the best of the now eight golf courses built alongside three hotels, a spa, and a sports facility at the Pinehurst Resort, designed by a man who became one of the most famous golf architects in the history of golf, Donald Ross. The most obvious characteristic of a Ross golf course is the green, which is often described as an upside-down cereal bowl.

6. TPC at Sawgrass, Ponte Vedra Beach, Florida — TPC stands for Tournament Player Club and consists of a chain of public and private golf courses operated by the PGA Tour (the PGA being the Professional Golfers Association, of course). TPC at Sawgrass was the inaugural Tournament Players Club and every golfer has seen a picture of its famous signature hole: The par-3, 132-yard 17th, known simply as the "Island Green," one of golf's most recognizable and difficult holes.

7. Torrey Pines Golf Course, San Diego, California — Torrey Pines is one of the finest municipal public golf courses in the United States, owned and operated by the city of San Diego. It sits on the coastal cliffs overlooking the Pacific Ocean in the suburb of La Jolla and is named after the Torrey Pine, a rare tree that grows in the wild only along this local stretch of the coastline in San Diego County.

8. Kingsbarns Golf Links, Kingsbarns, Fife, Scotland — Why do I include Kingsbarns Golfs Links in my list of golf courses you must know? Because it is my favorite course. Yep, that's right. After playing hundreds of golf courses all over the world, Kingsbarns captured my heart and is the subject of my daydreams on cold winter nights. What makes Kingsbarns so special to me is the way it captures the "feel" of Scotland: From the welcome brogue of the starter to its amphitheater effect (holes sloping toward the North Sea, which comes into view at every turn), it is magical, it is mystical, it is Scottish golf (which IS golf) at its best.

9. The Woodlands Club, Falmouth, Maine — What kind of member would I be if I did not include my home club, The Woodlands? Designed by the famous architectural team of George and Jim Fazio, it is simply the course I call "home." You have to be on top of your game to finish nine with the golf ball you began with, and if you can score less than a 7 on the toughest par 4 in the state of Maine (if not the world) — the number 4 hole with four ascending sand traps guarding the green — you can coast home from there!

NINE PLAYERS YOU SHOULD RECOGNIZE

No, you do not need to know who won the U.S. Open in 1960 (Arnold Palmer). But to be viewed as a golfer who has been around the links more than once, you need to recognize the names of the most important golfers who have played the game. Here's the Top Nine on my list!

1. Young Tom Morris *(April 20, 1851 – December 25, 1875)* — Young Tom Morris was the son of legendary golfer Old Tom Morris and he was also the Tiger Woods of the infant days of golf. He beat his champion father in a friendly match at the ripe old age of thirteen and went on to win four straight Open Championships, a feat that has never been duplicated. Tragically, Young Tom died at the age of twenty-four, heartbroken at the death of his wife and child during her birthing labor.

2. Jack Nicklaus *(born January 21, 1940)* — Jack is nicknamed "the Golden Bear" (because of his stout build and golden blond hair) and to this day he holds the record for winning the most major golf tournaments (eighteen). Unless or until Tiger Woods beats his record, Jack Nicklaus is likely to be considered the greatest golfer of all time (and maybe the best even if Tiger breaks his record). Jack is consistently among the longest and straightest hitters in the business and was known for his "course management," which means he planned his shots to manage risk and avoid trouble.

The "Golden Bear," Jack Nicklaus.

3. Eldrick "Tiger" Woods *(born December 30, 1975)* — Tiger could become the greatest golfer who ever played the game, although a sex scandal may derail him where his competitors could not. He won three straight U.S. Amateur titles before joining the PGA Tour. In 1997, at the age of twenty-two, he won the Masters by twelve strokes over his nearest competitor. To date, he has won fourteen majors and seventy-one PGA Tour events (only Sam Snead and Jack Nicklaus have won more PGA tournaments) and won the four majors in a row, although not in one calendar year. Tiger is known for his intense focus and mental toughness. He is also the first golfer to parallel the commitment to exercise and body building, made by athletes in other sports, to improve his strength and stamina.

4. Mildred "Babe" Didrikson Zaharias *(June 26, 1911 – September 27, 1956)* — No, not just the best female golfer of all time, but one of the top five golfers — male or female — of all time and, arguably, the greatest female athlete of all time. In 1939, *Time* magazine described her as the "1932 Olympic Games track and field star, expert basketball player, golfer, javelin thrower, hurdler, high jumper, swimmer, baseball pitcher, football halfback, billiardist, tumbler, boxer, wrestler, fencer, weight lifter, and adagio dancer." Babe didn't even take up golf until she was in her twenties and promptly won the first tournament she entered. She won seventeen of the eighteen tournaments she played in 1946 and 1947, and in her spare time she co-founded the Women's Professional Golf Association, the predecessor to the LPGA. Tragically, Babe died at the too-young age of forty-five.

5. Arnold Palmer *(born September 10, 1929)* — Nicknamed "The King," Arnold Palmer was the rock star of golf in the 1960s. Palmer is one of *the* most charismatic golfers, always engaging with his fans and interacting with the gallery. But he was no slouch on the golf course, winning sixty-one tournaments from 1954 through 1975. He was well known for aggressive play and "going for the hole" instead of ever playing safe and laying up.

The captain of "Arnie's Army," Arnold Palmer.

6. Ben Hogan *(August 13, 1912 – July 25, 1997)* — It has been said that Ben Hogan had the most perfect swing of any golfer who has played the game. His book, *Five Lessons: The Modern Fundamentals of Golf*, is one of the most widely read golf instruction books published. From 1938 through 1959, Hogan won sixty-three professional golf tournaments — particularly impressive when you consider that during this same period he also served in World War II and was involved in a near-fatal car accident.

7. Sam Snead *(May 27, 1912 – May 23, 2002)* — He only won seven major championships, but no golfer has ever won more PGA Tour events (eighty-two in all) than Sam Snead. Known as "Slammin' Sammy" (because of his long drives), Snead was also famous for a folksy demeanor and his quaint colloquial sayings.

8. Bobby Jones *(March 17, 1902 – December 18, 1971)* — Jones is the only player to have won the grand slam of golf (the four majors) in one calendar year (he eventually won thirteen majors). What is also amazing about Jones is that he could be considered one of the greatest golfers of all time even though he retired at age twenty-eight (to become a lawyer, of all things). He also co-designed the Augusta National course and founded the Masters Tournament. Ironically, Jones was never a professional golf player; he only competed as an amateur.

9. Annika Sorenstam *(born October 9, 1970)* — Born in Sweden, Annika was the female Tiger Woods during her professional career. Before retiring from competitive golf in 2008 at the ripe old age of thirty-eight, Annika had won more golf tournaments (ninety in all) than any other woman in history. She is also the only female golfer to have shot a 59 in competition and the first woman to play in a men's PGA Tour event since 1945 (the Bank of America Colonial tournament in 2003).

A JOKE TO TELL WHILE YOU'RE TEEING UP YOUR BALL.

SISTER MARY WALKS INTO THE OFFICE OF HER MOTHER SUPERIOR WITH A BENT HEAD AND SORROW IN HER EYES. "MOTHER SUPERIOR," SISTER MARY BEGINS, "I HAVE A CONFESSION TO MAKE TO YOU. I CURSED TODAY."

"YOU CURSED, SISTER MARY?" MOTHER SUPERIOR ASKS IN SURPRISE. "HOW DID THIS HAPPEN?"

"WELL I WAS PLAYING GOLF WITH SISTER ANNE. I WAS PLAYING PRETTY WELL, BUT ON THE SIXTH HOLE MY TEE SHOT HOOKED BADLY INTO THE WOODS."

"IS THAT WHEN YOU CURSED?" ASKS MOTHER SUPERIOR.

"OH, NO," REPLIES SISTER MARY. "ACTUALLY, THE BALL HIT A TREE AND BOUNCED INTO THE FAIRWAY. BUT THEN A HAWK SWOOPED DOWN AND PICKED UP THE BALL AND STARTED FLYING AWAY WITH IT."

"WELL, I CAN SEE HOW THAT COULD UPSET YOU," RESPONDS MOTHER SUPERIOR.

"ACTUALLY, THAT IS NOT WHY I CURSED," SAYS SISTER MARY. "THE BALL WAS OBVIOUSLY TOO HARD FOR THE HAWK TO HOLD ONTO AND IT DROPPED THE BALL RIGHT WHEN IT WAS FLYING OVER THE GREEN. THE BALL ROLLED ABOUT TWO FEET AWAY FROM THE PIN."

MOTHER SUPERIOR STARES AT SISTER MARY IN ICY SILENCE AND FINALLY SAYS, "AND YOU MISSED THE DAMN PUTT, DIDN'T YOU!"

Chapter 4

The Golf Commandments: Basic Golf Rules You Must Memorize

Golf is unique in that it is the only game in which the player calls a penalty on himself. This requires the player to be honest and to always do what is fair and right. Okay, that may not always happen, but I dare you to find a sport or game with more integrity than golf.

The rules of golf were created by the R&A, the organization that evolved from the Royal and Ancient Golf Club of St. Andrews, Scotland, the ruling authority for golf everywhere except the United States and Mexico. (The United States Golf Association, known as the USGA, works in tandem with the R&A to write and interpret the rules of golf for the U.S. and Mexico.) The R&A's official book, *The Rules of Golf,* states on the back cover that the basic underlying principle of golf is to play the course as you find it, play the ball as and where it lies, and if you cannot do either, do what is fair. Here is a short list of the rules you must absolutely know by heart and follow without deviation or hesitation.

BASIC ETIQUETTE

1. Don't talk when a player is hitting.
2. Play "ready golf." (The person farthest from the hole is traditionally required to hit first. However, modern golf requires that you play "ready golf," that is, keeping the game moving by hitting when you're ready if the person who is supposed to hit first is not ready to do so.)

3. Don't hit into a group in front of you.
4. Allow faster groups to "play through" your group (which means letting faster groups move ahead of you if you're playing at a slower pace).
5. Rake sand traps, repair divots on the golf course, and repair ball marks on the green.

BASIC RULES OF PLAY

1. Do not play with more than fourteen clubs.
2. Do not ask advice from anyone other than your partner or your caddie.
3. Do not give advice to anyone except your partner.

TEEING OFF

1. Your ball cannot be in front of, or outside of, the tee markers (your feet can be outside the tee box, but not your golf ball).

The ball must be teed up behind the two markers, but the golfer's forward foot can be in front of the line.

PLAYING THE BALL

1. As mentioned above, traditionally the player whose ball is farthest from the hole hits first. The winner of the hole tees off first on the next hole, which is called "having honors." However, under modern rules "ready golf" prevails: Play when ready if it does not endanger another player and if it is necessary to keep up the pace of play. And one more exception: If a golfer in your group makes a birdie or better, always let him tee off first whether you are ready to play or not.
2. Make sure you are playing your ball (which means know what ball you are playing).
3. Play the ball as it lies (in other words, do not move it or cause it to be moved).
4. Do not ground your club in a bunker or a hazard (your club should not touch the ground until it hits the ball).
5. Loose impediments (stones, leaves) as well as movable obstructions (rakes, tin cans) may be moved without penalty (so long as your ball doesn't move), but not in a sand trap or hazard.
6. If an immovable obstruction (water fountain, ball washer) interferes with your stance or swing, you may drop the ball without penalty within one club-length of the nearest point of relief as long as it's not nearer the hole.
7. If your ball is in a puddle (known as "casual water,") or in ground under repair, or in a hole made by a burrowing animal (or the footprint of the Abominable Snowman), you may drop it without penalty within one club-length of the nearest point of relief as long as it's not nearer the hole.
8. If you believe your ball is unplayable outside a hazard (and you are the sole judge of whether or not it is unplayable), you may take a drop with a one-stroke penalty.

Dropping your ball within two club-lengths of a hazard.

THE GOLF BALL

1. If a ball is moving, you may not touch it until it comes to a complete stop (and, yes, putting your foot in the way of a ball rolling back down a hill is touching the ball before it stops).

2. Never stop another player's ball.

3. When dropping a ball, hold it at shoulder height and arm's length and drop it. A drop in a situation with no penalty can be dropped one club-length; in a penalty situation, you get to drop it two club-lengths.

4. If a dropped ball strikes you, your partner, a caddie, or equipment, it can and must be redropped without penalty.

ON THE PUTTING GREEN

1. After marking your ball on the green you may pick it up, clean it, and replace it on the green precisely where it was.

2. Do not walk on the line of another player's putt (nothing, but nothing, will irritate other golfers more than you stomping all over the putting line).

3. Do not test the green by rolling your ball on the surface of the green prior to your putt.

4. If you are off the green, your ball can hit the flagstick without penalty; if you are on the green and your ball hits the flagstick it is a two-stroke penalty.
5. Assume that you must putt your ball until it is in the hole unless an opponent concedes the putt. In tournament play, a putt can only be conceded in match play, not stroke play.

A JOKE TO TELL WHILE YOU'RE TAKING SOME PRACTICE SWINGS.

BILL AND LARRY ARE OUT PLAYING GOLF ON A SUNNY TUESDAY AFTERNOON. LARRY SLICES THE BALL DEEP INTO A WOODED RAVINE. HE GRABS HIS 8-IRON AND SLIDES DOWN THE EMBANKMENT IN SEARCH OF HIS BALL.

THE GROUND COVER IS QUITE THICK, BUT A GLINT OF SUNLIGHT CATCHES HIS EYE. UPON FURTHER INVESTIGATION, LARRY REALIZES IT'S AN 8-IRON IN THE HANDS OF A SKELETON LYING NEXT TO AN OLD GOLF BALL.

LARRY IMMEDIATELY CALLS TO BILL, "COME QUICK, I'VE GOT TROUBLE DOWN HERE."

WHEN BILL GETS TO THE EDGE OF THE RAVINE HE SHOUTS DOWN, "WHAT'S THE MATTER, LARRY?"

LARRY YELLS BACK, "THROW ME MY 7-IRON. YOU CAN'T GET OUT OF HERE WITH AN 8-IRON."

Chapter 5

Would You Join a Club That Would Have Me as a Member? Golf Organizations and Tournaments You Should Know

THE GOLF ORGANIZATIONS

You may never become a professional golfer, but you can still belong to a golfing association and journey to see the professionals play in the tournaments they sponsor.

1. Professional Golf Association of America (the PGA of America)
Just call it the PGA. It was founded in 1916 and is the largest sports organization in the world, with 28,000 men and women golf professionals. You cannot join the PGA unless you are a professional, but you will want to watch many PGA-sponsored tournaments, particularly the PGA Championship, the final major of the season.
www.pga.com

2. United States Golf Association (USGA)
The USGA is the governing body for golf in the United States and Mexico. It provides the national handicap system for golfers, conducts thirteen national championships (including the U.S. Open, U.S. Women's Open, and U.S. Senior Open), and tests golf equipment to ensure conformance with regulations. This is an organization you can and

should join. Membership dues are minimal, you get a hat, bag tag, and a small book with the rules of golf, and you can say you belong to the same organization that would have me as a member!
www.usga.org

3. The R&A
Formerly known as the Royal and Ancient Golf Club of St. Andrews, this organization is the equivalent of the USGA everywhere except the United States and Mexico. This is not an organization you can join, but it is one you must know about, because it was the first, and is still the foremost, authority on golf and golf rules in the world.
http://www.randa.org/

THE GOLF TOURNAMENTS

There are hundreds of golf tournaments throughout the world throughout the year. However, if you do not know about, recognize, keep track of, and watch the following tournaments, you will be mistaken for an amateur bowler instead of a golfer.

1. The Masters — The Masters is the first of the four annual international golf tournaments that, today, constitute the "majors." It is played in the first full week of April and is the only major held each year at the same location: The Augusta National Golf Club in Augusta, Georgia. The Masters was co-founded by the great Bobby Jones, who designed Augusta National with course architect Alister MacKenzie. The field of players is smaller than those of the other major championships because it is by invitation only, entry being controlled by the Augusta National

Golf Club. As mentioned earlier, the Masters champion is given a green jacket to wear throughout his championship year (to be returned when the next champion is crowned).

2. The U.S. Open — Any golfer (professional or amateur) who has a handicap index of 1.4 or lower may attempt to qualify for the U.S. Open. Many professional golfers are exempt from qualifying, based on world rankings and performances at previous tournaments, but thousands of golfers attempt to qualify each year at local qualifying events. The U.S. Open is the second of the majors, and is scheduled by the USGA to take place in mid-June, so that the final round (assuming no unforeseen weather delays) is played on Father's Day Sunday.

3. The Open Championship — The Open Championship is known to Americans as the British Open, but in Europe it is referred to simply as The Open. It is the third and oldest of the four majors and it is the only major held outside the United States (on one of nine historic links courses in Scotland or England). It is administered by the R&A, the organization that superseded the Royal and Ancient Golf Club of St. Andrews in 2004.

4. The PGA Championship — The PGA Championship (sometimes referred to as the U.S. PGA Championship outside North America) is the fourth, and final, of the majors and is conducted by the PGA of America as part of the PGA Tour. It is usually played in mid-August (customarily four weeks after the British Open). The winner of the PGA Championship is automatically invited to play in the other three majors for the next five years and is exempt from qualifying for the PGA Championship for life. The winner also receives membership on the PGA Tour and invitations to the Players Championship for five years. Not to mention the $1.3 million-plus purse.

5. The Ryder Cup Matches — This is a competition between a European team and a team from the United States. The competition is jointly administered by the PGA of America and the PGA European Tour, and is held every two years, with the venue alternating between courses in the United States and Europe. Early matches between the two sides were fairly even, but after the Second World War, repeated dominance by the United States led to a 1979 decision to extend the representation of the British and Irish team to include players from continental Europe. Following this change the event became much more competitive, with both Europe and America winning the Ryder Cup seven times each.

6. The Presidents Cup — This tournament is identical to the Ryder Cup, except it is between a team representing the United States and a team of international golfers from anywhere other than Europe. The Presidents Cup alternates with the Ryder Cup, both tournaments being held every two years.

7. The FedEx Cup — The PGA Tour was organized in 1968 (when a group of tour professionals split off from the PGA) and crowns its champion with the FedEx Cup. Announced in 2005 and first awarded in 2007, it is the first (and currently only) playoff system in men's professional golf. Throughout the year, golfers earn points for winning various PGA Tour golf tournaments, culminating in a final series of elimination tournaments at the end of each year. Oh, by the way, the winner of the FedEx Cup earns a paltry $10 million of the $35 million prize fund.

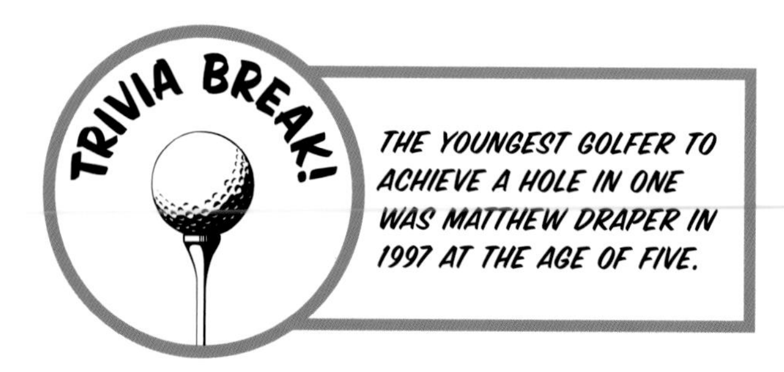

A JOKE TO TELL WHILE YOU ARE FISHING YOUR BALL OUT OF THE POND.

A HUSBAND RELUCTANTLY AGREED TO PLAY IN THE COUPLES' ALTERNATE-SHOT TOURNAMENT AT HIS CLUB. HE TEED OFF ON THE FIRST HOLE, A PAR 4, AND BLISTERED A DRIVE 300 YARDS DOWN THE MIDDLE OF THE FAIRWAY. UPON REACHING THE BALL, THE HUSBAND SAID TO HIS WIFE, "JUST HIT IT TOWARD THE GREEN, ANYWHERE AROUND THERE WILL BE FINE."

THE WIFE PROCEEDED TO SHANK THE BALL DEEP INTO THE WOODS.

UNDAUNTED, THE HUSBAND SAID, "THAT'S OKAY, SWEETHEART," AND SPENT FIVE FULL MINUTES LOOKING FOR THE BALL. HE FOUND IT JUST IN TIME, BUT IN A HORRIBLE POSITION. HE PLAYED THE SHOT OF HIS LIFE TO GET THE BALL WITHIN TWO FEET OF THE HOLE. HE TOLD HIS WIFE TO KNOCK THE BALL IN.

HIS WIFE THEN PROCEEDED TO KNOCK THE BALL OFF THE GREEN AND INTO A BUNKER. STILL MAINTAINING HIS COMPOSURE, THE HUSBAND SUMMONED ALL OF HIS SKILL AND HOLED THE SHOT FROM THE BUNKER.

HE TOOK THE BALL OUT OF THE HOLE AND, WHILE WALKING OFF THE GREEN, PUT HIS ARM AROUND HIS WIFE AND CALMLY SAID, "HONEY, THAT WAS A BOGEY-5, AND THAT'S OKAY, BUT I THINK WE CAN DO BETTER ON THE NEXT HOLE."

TO WHICH SHE REPLIED, "LISTEN, DON'T BITCH AT ME. ONLY TWO OF THOSE FIVE SHOTS WERE MINE."

Chapter 6

Golf Magazines, Books, and Movies You Must Read or Watch

GOLF MAGAZINES YOU SHOULD SUBSCRIBE TO

Obviously, I love to play golf. Although I prefer playing golf to reading about it, there are those days when two feet of snow inhibit even me from hitting the links. How to while away the hours waiting for spring? By reading my favorite golf magazines cover to cover.

Golf Digest

Golf Digest is the number-one golf publication in the world. My favorite section of *Golf Digest* is "Local Knowledge," which answers questions about rules and gives you playing guidelines.
www.golf.com

Golf Magazine

Golf Magazine is very similar to *Golf Digest*. My favorite section of *Golf Magazine* is "Ask Travelin' Joe," which gives readers tips about golf and travel. *www.golfmagazine.com*

Golf Illustrated

Golf Illustrated is the oldest golf publication in the United States, having first been published in 1914. Its primary focus is instruction.
www.golfillustrated.com

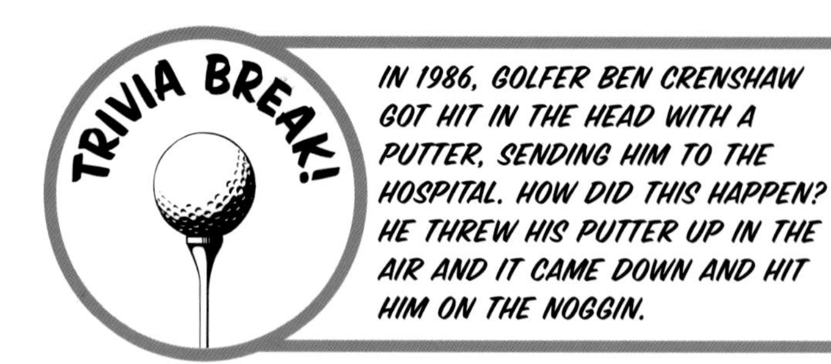

GOLF BOOKS YOU MUST READ

1. *Harvey Penick's Little Red Book* —This book is generally considered the "bible" of golf reading. Harvey Penick is a legendary golf instructor from Austin,Texas, who wrote down random golf instructional "thoughts" in a little red notebook throughout his long teaching tenure.Then, at age eighty-seven, he decided to share his observations with the rest of the world. It's a relatively short book (175 pages), but it delivers tips and advice in such a pithy manner that you will read it once a year. (Published by Simon & Schuster.)

2. *Five Lessons: The Modern Fundamentals of Golf* by Ben Hogan — It has been said that Ben Hogan had the most perfect swing of any golfer who has played the game.This book gives you his five basic lessons of the golf swing. (Published by Fireside Books.)

3. *Golf My Way* by Jack Nicklaus — Just reading about how this great player approaches and analyzes the game of golf will fascinate you, even if you never attempt to duplicate any aspect of his swing. (Published by Simon & Schuster.)

4. *Extraordinary Golf* by Fred Shoemaker — While you will not see this book on most lists of great golf books, I found it to be the best book on how to enjoy the game of golf.This is not a book about the mechanics of perfecting your game; it's an inspiring look at how to enjoy what you are doing. (Published by Perigee Books.)

GOLF MOVIES EVEN YOUR SPOUSE WILL LIKE

1. *Caddyshack* — No golfer should ever die without seeing *Caddyshack*, which stars Chevy Chase, Bill Murray, and Rodney Dangerfield. You will not learn how to play golf watching the movie, but it will reinforce the philosophy that if you are not having fun playing, you don't understand what the game is all about.

2. *The Legend of Bagger Vance* —This movie has so many lessons about the philosophy of golf it bears repeated viewing. Starring Will Smith and Matt Damon, it explores both the arrogance and humility of golfers and how, sometimes, you have to "let go" of your baggage to live your life (or play your game).

3. *Tin Cup* —This is another movie that perfectly exemplifies the spirit of the game. Starring Kevin Costner and Rene Russo, it shows how anyone can qualify for the U.S. Open and it compares playing safe versus "going for it" without caring if you win or lose.

A JOKE TO TELL WHILE YOU'RE FIXING A BALL MARK ON THE GREEN.

JESUS AND PETER ARE PLAYING A ROUND OF GOLF. PETER STEPS UP TO THE TEE OF A PAR 3 AND HITS A BEAUTIFUL SHOT, LONG AND STRAIGHT, LANDING TEN FEET FROM THE PIN.

IT'S JESUS' TURN. HE TEES IT UP AND HOOKS IT BADLY, RIGHT INTO TRAFFIC. IT HITS THE BUMPER OF A CAR AND BOUNCES INTO A GUTTER. A FROG JUMPS OUT OF THE GUTTER WITH THE BALL AND STARTS HOPPING AWAY. A HAWK SWOOPS DOWN AND GRABS THE FROG WITH THE BALL IN ITS MOUTH AND STARTS FLYING OVER THE GOLF COURSE. RIGHT WHEN THE HAWK REACHES THE HOLE THE FROG CROAKS AND THE BALL DROPS RIGHT INTO THE HOLE.

PETER TURNS TO JESUS AND SAYS, "STOP SCREWING AROUND. THIS IS FOR MONEY."

Chapter 7

Gearing Up for Success: Golf Equipment and Accessories

There are golf necessities, golf accessories, and golf gimmicks. Follow me as I search through my golf bag and provide you with the basics about every toy waiting for your enjoyment.

MUST-HAVES

We will discuss bags, clubs, and balls in-depth in the upcoming chapters, but here's an overview of what you need to know about golf equipment. If you don't understand a particular term, don't worry — it will be covered later!

GOLF BAG

You need one. It's much easier to carry fourteen clubs in a bag than under your arm.

CLUBS

You need fourteen. Well, you probably need more than fourteen, but the rules of golf only allow you to carry fourteen clubs in your bag (and that includes your putter, which, of course, is a club). You can have fewer than fourteen (not that I have ever come up with a reason why you would want fewer than the fourteen you are allowed), but you can never, never, never have more than fourteen. Competitors will count, so don't forget to remove that extra driver you took to the driving range just to try out before you start to play.

There's no requirement as to what fourteen clubs you choose. You can have nine wedges, three putters, and two drivers, so long as you don't have any more clubs than these. But that would be an eclectic collection of sticks. The typical bag of the twenty-first century includes a driver, a fairway wood (could be, but doesn't have to be, a 3-wood), a hybrid or "rescue club" (a relatively new creation designed to assist our ability to hit out of a rough), a putter, one to three wedges, and the remaining clubs are irons, ranging from a 1-iron to a 10-iron. I have never seen a one iron and I have only seen one 2-iron. In the recent past, most golfers had a 3-iron through 10-iron as their basic set, but the lower-numbered clubs (3- and even 4-irons) are now often replaced by a hybrid club or removed to make room for more wedges. And just so you know, the 10-iron is often interchangeable with a pitching wedge.

What's in my bag (which solely suits me): King Cobra driver, King Cobra 3-wood, 15.5-degree Cleveland hybrid, 4-iron through 10-iron, three wedges (52, 56, and 60 degrees — gap, sand, and lob, which I'll discuss in greater detail later), and my trusty Odyssey White Hot 2 Ball putter. I have exchanged my hybrid with a 3-iron when the hybrid wasn't working for me. Likewise, I have often used my old Callaway Steelhead 4-wood when my 3-wood was acting up. The point is to pick out the fourteen clubs you want and then you should feel free to exchange them at will, so long as you don't do so during a round.

GOLF BALLS

It is very hard to play golf without golf balls. I always have as many balls as will comfortably fit in the compartment made for the balls in my bag — typically not fewer than eighteen. I figure I won't lose more than one golf ball a hole during an eighteen-hole round, and if I am headed in that direction I should probably stop playing after my eighteenth golf ball is lost anyway.

TEES

A tee is a wooden or plastic object that is pushed into the ground and it is used to elevate your ball before you hit it. This may seem obvious, but you can only use a tee on your drive. As you would expect, there are all sorts of different colors and sizes of tees. What is most important is the height of a tee. Longer tees (3 to 3.5 inches) allow you to position the ball higher off the ground and are generally used for today's modern woods. Shorter tees (1.5 to 2.5 inches) are suitable for irons and are more easily inserted and less easily broken than long tees. Of course, you can make a long tee shorter by simply inserting it further into the ground, so don't feel you have to carry tees of different lengths. By the way, if you want an interesting tidbit of trivia, the rules of golf actually allow for a mound of sand to be used as a tee. But don't do that. That would be showing off and you'll have plenty of time to prove your prowess hitting out of a sand trap. Also, if your tee breaks when you hit your ball (a frequent occurrence) pick it up and discard it either in a box by the tee provided for broken tees or the next time you see a waste receptacle. Broken tees wreak havoc on lawn mowers.

The tee box is the only time or place you can hit your ball from a tee.

Rabid golfers see golf balls whenever they look.

BALL MARKERS

This is different from making a mark on your ball so you will recognize and play your ball when you find it (hopefully) on the fairway. Ball markers are used for marking where your golf ball is on the green when you pick it up to either clean it or to get it out of the way of another putt. It is legal in golf to pick up your ball from the green to clean it, admire it, or do anything else you wish to do with it (to kiss it for good luck, for example). However, you have to mark the location of the ball on the green before you pick it up. Typically, a golf ball marker is any flat, round item that you can see from a distance after you have marked your ball and walked around the green. It is embarrassing if you have marked your ball and you need your partners to help you find the marker. One of my favorite golfing partners, Jim McLaren from South Carolina, gave me a ball marker from the Masters. Using a marker that reminds you of a pal or a favorite golf course just makes your round all the more enjoyable.

You always put the mark behind the ball, not in front or to the side of it. There are also some ball markers that clip onto a ball marker repair tool and some that clip onto a golf hat. Just remember that in a pinch a quarter will do.

GOLF GLOVES

Although you are not required to do so, most golfers wear a glove when playing golf. If you are right-handed you will wear a glove on your left hand and, of course, if you are left-handed you will wear a glove on your right hand. Wearing gloves will prevent calluses from forming on your hand and will provide you with a better grip on your club so it won't accidentally slip out of your hands if you are sweating. You will miss hitting your ball properly if your club slips during your swing. And it could be a disaster for another golfer if the club slips out of your hands completely. You can wear a glove on both hands, but that is overkill and unusual. There are special golf gloves to wear in the rain or cold weather and those would be worn in pairs rather than just on one hand. And keep in mind that, with the relatively high price you can pay for golf clubs, don't go cheap when it comes to golf gloves. You don't have to buy an expensive golf glove, but buy a new one when yours gets worn out or stretched out. I actually use three golf gloves when I play. I rotate through each one of them one-third of the way through my round. This actually results in all three gloves lasting longer and never stretching out.

GOLF SHOES

Playing golf in loafers is not a good idea. Your feet need to grip the ground when you swing your club. That is why you need golf shoes. Golf shoes have spikes on their soles to grip the ground as you deliver your mighty blow to the little white globe awaiting deliverance. A decade ago, every golfer had steel spikes on their golf shoes. However, steel spikes caused significant damage to greens, so most of today's courses have banned steel spikes and restrict you to plastic-spiked golf shoes. Fortunately, those are the kind of shoes you can find in every golf store in the world. The downside to plastic spikes is that they wear down fairly quickly. But it is very easy to buy and install replacement spikes (or virtually any pro shop will do it for you). Replace your spikes before you start slipping on your backswing. By the way, if you are in a pinch (your buddy just happens to call you while your boss is out of town and suggests a quick round) you can play in sneakers, although you are likely to slide without spikes, particularly if the ground is wet. And just so you don't think all golf shoes are boring, today you can buy sneakers with golf spikes built into them, and you can even buy sandals made specifically to play golf. It was a ton of fun the first time I wore golf sandals to play golf and the pro shop told me spiked shoes were required. I showed him the sole of my sandals punctuated by golf spikes and I was off to the first tee. When selecting golf shoes, go for the newer and readily available lightweight golf shoes. If you are going to walk and lug around a bag filled with iron, not having to trudge along in heavy golf shoes will dramatically reduce your fatigue.

BALL MARK REPAIR TOOL

You should always have a ball mark repair tool and you should always repair any dent your ball may leave on a green. It's also a nice touch to repair a pitch mark some other golfer left unrepaired because he was too narcissistic to take the

Always repair your ball mark (and any other ones you find) on the green.

three seconds needed to take care of his own mark. And just to make sure I am not talking about you, repair your ball mark! Most pro shops will give you a repair tool, although you can also buy elaborate repair tools that may also have a ball marker built into them. And as is true about ball markers, you can use a repair tool of sentimental value. My college roommate, Dave Osher, gave me an ancient University of Michigan combination repair tool and ball marker that reminds me of those good ole college days.

IDENTIFICATION TAGS

Many golf courses have name tags for golf bags that identify the course and include a place for you to write your name (or the club will print your name on the tag for you). Some golfers actually save these for their home collection of golf mementos. There are other sensible reasons to have bag tags: If you play at a club at which an attendant takes your bag from the bag drop, then having an identification tag for your bag will help ensure that he'll put it in the cart assigned to you for your round; it is also possible that someone could pick up the wrong bag of clubs, so a name tag gives you additional protection.

SHOULD-HAVES

TOWELS

Most golf bags have a ring to which you can attach a golf towel and most golf shops have golf towels that have a hook that allows you to attach the towel to your bag. Just made for each other. However, I will be honest with you: Every time I attach my towel to the golf bag ring it eventually gets ripped off. I step on it or catch it in the trunk of my car. But that's just me. I still have a towel, but I keep it in one of the golf bag compartments instead of attached to the outside. The towels that have hooks in the middle instead of a corner drape a shorter distance and are less likely to catch on a foreign object.

BALL RETRIEVERS

Ball retrievers are telescoping poles with a device at the end that traps and scoops up golf balls, and are typically used to get a ball out of a water hazard. It is fine for you to attempt to retrieve your ball from the water. It is even financially beneficial to attempt to retrieve balls left in the water by other golfers. But retrieving golf balls is not analogous to fishing. You can't wait all day for the golf ball to jump into your ball retriever. If you see your ball and you can retrieve it quickly and easily, go for it. If a few others are also within sight, all the better. But don't hold up the group behind you and, for goodness' sake, don't fall into the water stretching for a distant ball.

GOLF UMBRELLA

It's no fun playing in the rain, but there will be times when the sun will be shining and there won't be a cloud in the sky when you tee off and yet, by the thirteenth hole, you'll be getting drenched. So I always have a golf umbrella in my bag. Not a small, collapsible umbrella, but a big, broad umbrella that will at least keep my head and the upper part of my body dry. Remember that the umbrella will only keep you dry if it's over your head. You can't swing a club while holding an umbrella, so if you decide to play in the rain your umbrella will only be useful between shots. In those cases, I tend to use my umbrella to keep my clubs dry instead of me. There is actually a small umbrella you can buy to put in your bag and it opens up just to keep your clubs dry. The one I have actually has a ball retriever on the end of it. The better golf courses have golf carts with back panels that will pull down and cover your golf clubs to keep them relatively dry if a sudden downpour surprises you.

Betty Boop will keep an eye on your ball.

GOLF CLUB HEAD COVERS

These keep your clubs protected and looking relatively unscathed. Golf head covers are used primarily for woods or hybrids, not for irons. You can buy them for irons but, frankly, let me be honest with you: If you use iron covers you will be considered a golf nerd. Don't do it. You'll get too lazy to take them off and put them on after every shot anyway and you really don't want to hear snickering behind your back, do you? Ironically, although using iron head covers will be viewed as nerdy, you can use a variety of silly covers for your drivers without any ridicule at all. Tiger Woods has a tiger for a head cover (I assume you can figure out the connection). One of my golfing partners has a poodle head cover, because he loves his dogs. I have a set of University of Michigan head covers because, of course, I am a rabid U-M alumnus (is there any other kind?). It also allows me to refuse to play with anyone who has an Ohio State golf club cover. Okay, just kidding. The point is a cute head cover is cool and iron head covers are not. Don't ask me why. It's just the way it is.

SUNGLASSES

Following recent advances in technology, today's sunglass manufacturers now produce sunglasses specifically for golf. Some lenses are designed to enhance your view of the contours of a green. Some golf sunglasses wrap around your face so that when you are bending over your putt the sun doesn't blind you from the side. This is well worth the investment because curved sunglasses generally give you a better perspective of the curves on a green than do flat sunglasses.

SUNBLOCK

I am not a doctor but I know the risks of skin cancer. And in a round of golf I know I'll be out in the sun for four to five hours, so I always have a bottle of sunblock in my bag. How excited will you be with a round of 95 if you also get a blistering sunburn? Want to guess which one you'll be thinking about the next morning? I advise putting the sunblock on before you leave your house. That way you can make sure you thoroughly wash your hands, avoiding a greasy hold on your clubs that would result from applying the lotion on the first tee.

INSECT REPELLANT

If you play golf in Maine in June you will meet our state insect — the black fly. Presumably, if you play elsewhere you will meet your own state insect, such as mosquitoes, ticks, and gnats. Insect repellant is in my bag right next to the sunblock. It's not easy swinging a club while swatting away insects.

GOLF CLUB BRUSH

You can buy a tool that looks very much like a toothbrush to scrub your clubs periodically. Just as plaque builds up on your teeth, you'll find that dirt, sand, and grime build up on your golf clubs and they can affect the spin of your golf ball. Golf club brushes have steel or plastic bristles to clean the grooves of your clubs. I typically don't clean my clubs with a brush during the round, but don't let me stop you from being fastidious. A clean club is certainly more accurate than one in which the grooves are filled with dirt. The golf club brush usually has a hook that allows you to attach it to the same ring on your golf bag designed to hold your golf towel.

FUN-TO-HAVES

GOLF CARTS

No, I'm not talking about a battery-operated riding cart (although having one in which to tool around your neighborhood would be cool). I am talking about a pullcart or pushcart. Unmotorized. A walking golf cart. If you like to walk, but you don't like to carry your clubs, a walking golf cart is the ticket for you. Ten years ago the typical walking golf cart had two wheels and two plastic semi-circular holders to rest the bag on. You pulled your clubs behind you and there you went. Although those carts still exist, some chiropractor figured out that twisting your body to pull your clubs may not enhance your back or your golf game. So today you can find a three-wheeled cart that you push rather than pull. I use a push cart because I am somewhat lazy. I even have a battery-operated push cart that works similarly to a power lawn mower: You control it more than push it and off you go. By the way, you can spend a couple of thousand dollars for a cart that uses a laser to follow you around the golf course, but let's not get carried away here. Virtually all golf courses rent pushcarts or pullcarts at a very low cost.

TRIVIA BREAK!

THE WORLD'S HIGHEST GOLF COURSE IS THE TACTU GOLF CLUB IN MOROCOCHA, PERU. IT SITS 14,335 FEET ABOVE SEA LEVEL AT ITS LOWEST POINT.

RANGEFINDERS

A rangefinder is a device that will tell you the distance from your ball to either the flag or the middle of the green. There are some very inexpensive viewfinders that purport to tell you the distance to the green based on elevations. I do not find these very reliable. You could probably eyeball the distance just as easily. There are more expensive "laser rangefinders" that latch onto a flagstick and use a laser to determine your distance. I have tried these, but because I have difficulty keeping my hands steady, using them became a chore. With the onslaught of GPS tracking devices for your car, it didn't take very long for these devices to find their way onto the golf course. A few years ago, it was illegal to use a GPS during a round of golf. However, since golf pros spend hours prior to a tournament measuring distances from landmarks to the center of the green, the golf gurus in charge of the rules finally gave us a break and allowed the assistance of rangefinders. But not all the time: In a tournament, local club rules apply so make sure you check with the pro before pulling out your rangefinder.

Many of the newer electric golf carts have a built-in GPS tracking device that will tell you how far your cart is from the center of the green. It will also yell at you when you go off the cart path on a par 3. I guess you have to sacrifice a little privacy for the certainty of distance.

STROKE COUNTERS

If you have difficulty remembering how many strokes you have taken (although I guarantee you that your playing partner will know) there are stroke counters that you can use to help you keep track. Just click the counter every time you take a stroke to record the number of strokes you took on a hole or the entire round. Of course, you can just ask your partner. Nerd warning: If you pull out a stroke counter you will hear snickering behind your back. It is not hard to keep your score on every hole, and once you write it down on your scorecard it is off to the next hole. When does it become complicated? When you hit your ball out of bounds or in a hazard.

Once again, remember that golf is suppose to be fun. And what could possibly make a game more fun than toys and gadgets that you can play with during your round? These items enhance the enjoyment of your game and golfers always compete to have the latest toy to show off to their playing buddies.

A JOKE TO TELL WHILE YOU'RE CLEANING YOUR CLUB.

TONY WAS ALREADY SHOOTING WELL OVER 50 WHEN HE REACHED THE PAR-3 SEVENTH HOLE. AFTER DRIVING TWO BALLS INTO THE WATER AND ONE OUT OF THE SAND TRAP, HE LINED UP TO PUTT THE NINE FEET TO THE HOLE. DURING HIS BACK SWING HIS CADDY COUGHED. TONY WENT NUTS AND SAID, "YOU HAVE GOT TO BE THE WORST CADDY IN THE WORLD."

"I DOUBT IT," REPLIED THE CADDY. "THAT WOULD BE TOO MUCH OF A COINCIDENCE."

Chapter 8

Is That a Putter in Your Bag or Are You Just Happy to Be Playing Golf?

GOLF CLUBS

Now that you know you are limited to fourteen clubs in your bag, which ones should you choose and why?

WOODS

Woods are the clubs designed to hit your ball the longest distance possible. The primary wood is your driver. Today's driver typically has a very large head and, as is true of all woods, has a long shaft for maximum club speed. Historically, woods were made from persimmon wood. In 1979, TaylorMade Golf introduced the first metal "wood," made of steel. The construction of clubs evolved quickly from that point, and manufacturers are now using materials such as carbon fiber, titanium, and scandium. So today's woods do not have a speck of wood in them. Not even a sliver. But we still call them woods because, after all, golf is a game of tradition.

Every golf club has a different "loft." Loft is the angle of the clubface to the shaft and this angle controls trajectory which, of course, affects distance. Think about it this way: More loft logically makes a ball go higher, thus a shorter distance, even though we are talking in degrees, not inches. A driver has a loft between 7 and 12 degrees. Professional golfers typically use lower-lofted drivers (less than 10 degrees of loft) because the ball goes farther even though it takes a more precise swing to hit the ball correctly. Most beginning and average golfers use drivers with a loft of 9 to 12 degrees.

The driver is your largest and longest club in your bag.

There are as many different types of shafts as there are heads and grips. Every shaft has a different "flex" to it. When you swing your club at a ball the shaft actually bends; the flex is the degree to which the shaft will bend when the club is swung at the ball. There are five ratings usually used for shaft flex: extra stiff, stiff, regular, senior, and ladies (sorry, women, this sexist term is not mine), usually denoted by the letters X, S, R, A, and L ("A" is used for senior because this flex was originally called "amateur"). The reason why flex is important is because if it doesn't match your swing, the clubface will be misaligned at impact, causing your shots to go off-target.

The faster your swing, the stiffer the shaft necessary to keep your club aligned properly. But since it's harder to time how fast your swing is, you can also predict the appropriate flex for the shaft based on the distance of your drive. If you can hit a ball on your drive an average of 250 yards or more (will you play with me?) you would use a stiff shaft; if your average is 230 - 250 yards, use a regular shaft; if it's 200 - 230 yards, use a senior shaft; and if it's less than 200 yards, use a ladies' shaft. Only the biggest of the big hitters should use an extra stiff shaft.

The grip of the club is connected to the shaft, which is connected to the clubhead, which completes the entire golf club. This kind of "grip" is different from your partner telling you to "get a grip on yourself." That just means you're losing your concentration, not your club. The grip is the top section of the club that you wrap your hands around to swing your club. The grip is essential, because without it you will lose your grip on your club.

According to the rules of golf, all club grips, with the exception of the putter, must have a circular cross-section. Bet you didn't even notice that, did you? Grips may taper from thick to thin along their length (and virtually all do), but they are not allowed to have any waisting (a thinner section of the grip surrounded by thicker sections above and below it) or bulges (the opposite of waisting — thicker sections of the grip surrounded by thinner sections).

Do not underestimate the importance of the grip of your club. If your grip does not have "tack" (as opposed to you having "tact") your club could easily slip as you are swinging it. I treat myself to having my clubs regripped every winter. Virtually every golf store will replace your grips for you at a very low cost (this may vary according to quality, but you are still looking at under $100.00 to change the grips of all of your clubs).

Back to woods. The driver is, logically, the 1-wood. After the driver you can have woods ranging from a 2-wood to an 11- wood, although in recent years it has been hard to find even-numbered woods. Typically, you will see a 3-, 5-, 7-, 9-, or 11-wood. The 3- and 5-woods are the most common woods you will find in play.

The higher the number of the golf club, the higher the loft. Also, the higher the golf club number, the shorter the shaft of the club. Finally, the higher the golf club number the less distance you can expect to hit your ball with that club (think of it in terms of the following equation: higher loft = higher shot = less distance.)

As I mentioned above, the loft of the driver is between 7 and 12 degrees. A 3-wood has a loft between 15 and 18 degrees and a 5-wood has a loft between 20 and 22 degrees. A 3-wood is generally one-half-inch shorter than a driver, and so on with each successive club.

Now to get just a little bit more complicated: Some of the higher-numbered woods will have the same degree of loft as some of the lower-numbered irons (both would thus have the same trajectory and would presumably hit the ball the same distance). This explains the decrease in popularity of some of the lower-numbered irons, because the higher-numbered woods are easier for the average golfer to hit than the lower-numbered irons. For example, the 7-wood and the 4-iron typically have the same degree of loft (25 - 28), but most golfers find the 7-wood easier to hit than the 4-iron.

Just so you know the terminology, the 3- and 5-woods are also referred to as "fairway woods" because they are most often used for your second shot of each hole and, hopefully, you are on the fairway when you are hitting your second shot. The higher-lofted woods (7, 9, 11, and, by the way, there are some companies that manufacture woods even higher than the 11) are known as "utility woods."

IRONS

Irons were designed for shots approaching the green or from more difficult lies, such as the rough, the base of hills or through or over trees. Because each higher-numbered iron will presumably go less distance (but higher in the air if you want to get over that tree), the closer you are to the green, the higher the iron you'll want to use. Historically, a standard set of irons consisted of a 3-, 4-, 5-, 6-, 7-, 8-, and 9-iron, plus the pitching wedge (which could also be the 10-iron). Because the lower-numbered irons (the 3 and 4) are harder to hit than higher-numbered utility woods, many of today's sets of irons start with the 4-iron.

As with woods, "irons" get their name because they were, duh, originally made from forged iron.

TRIVIA BREAK!

IN 1586, THE FIRST WOMAN WAS ALLOWED TO PLAY GOLF. WHO WAS SHE? MARY STUART, THE QUEEN OF SCOTLAND.

And just as there are different kinds of woods, there are different kinds of irons. You can have hybrids, cavity-back, or muscle-back irons. A hybrid is any iron that has a head similar to a fairway wood, but it's typically smaller with a shorter-length shaft. A cavity-back iron is any iron in which there is a cavity carved out of the back of the head of the club. This allows the weight of the club to be distributed around the perimeter of the club instead of right smack dab in the middle of the head. A muscle-back iron is the opposite of the cavity-back iron: There is no cavity on the back of the head, so the weight is more evenly distributed across the back of the clubhead. If you hit with a muscle-back iron, you have to hit the ball in the center of the club for it to go the distance and in the direction you desire. Cavity-back irons are more forgiving, which means if you hit it off center you won't lose as much distance because there is a larger area of weighted contact on the clubhead.

A cavity-back iron distributes the weight of the club around the perimeter.

How far does the average ball travel with each iron wielded by the average golfer? The average golfer hits his 5-iron approximately 160 yards. Why do I only mention the distance from this one club? Because it is easier to describe the distance of each successive club once you know the distance you hit using one club. As a general rule, the lower the number of your iron, the farther the average distance it will hit the ball. Therefore, each successive club goes approximately ten yards farther or ten yards shorter, depending on which way up or down the ladder you're heading. So if your 5-iron goes 160 yards, your 4-iron will probably go 170 yards and your 3-iron 180 yards. Going the other direction, your 6-iron will go 150 yards, your 7-iron 140 yards, and so on. These numbers are not etched in stone, so if your 7-iron goes 130 yards it does not mean you're a weakling. It just means you may need to adjust your choice of club based on how far from the flag you are. That is why knowing the distance to the center of the green is so critical to your golf game.

Once you get past your 10-iron (or pitching wedge), each successive wedge will travel approximately twenty yards less than the one before it. As a rule of thumb, it's good to remember: Don't cling to numbers, but use them as a guide.

WEDGES

Wedges are irons, but they are unique irons. They have the highest lofts of all of the irons, which means they go higher but travel less distance. Based on the distances mentioned above, an average gap wedge will go 95 yards, the sand wedge (thank you Gene Sarazen) 75 yards, and the lob wedge 55 yards.

There are actually six types of wedges, with lofts ranging from 45 degrees to 64 degrees, but the four most common wedges are: 1) the pitching wedge (you will see either a P or the number 10 on the club) with a loft of 48 degrees; 2) the gap wedge (GW on the club, or it may be labeled AW or UW because it used to be called an approach wedge or utility wedge) with a loft of 52 degrees; 3) the sand wedge (SW) with a loft of 56 degrees; and 4) the lob wedge (LW) with a loft of 60 degrees.

The sand wedge is self explanatory — it is typically used to get out of the sand trap and is designed to do so by having the widest sole (bottom edge) of any wedge, which provides the greatest amount of bounce to the club. Bounce? What is bounce you ask? Simple: On most other irons, the sole of the club is perpendicular to the shaft, meaning it is roughly parallel to the ground when the club is at rest, allowing the leading edge to get between the ball and the ground more easily. However, the sand wedge is designed with the sole of the club at an angle to the ground, lifting the leading edge of the club off the ground and allowing the club to slide through the sand more easily. Or that's the theory anyway. Since it has been in use since 1932, it seems to have worked pretty well for those in the know.

Since the pitching wedge has a loft of 48 degrees and the sand wedge has one of 56 degrees, we needed something to fill the "gap" between them. Thus, was born the gap wedge! And the lob wedge just has the highest loft of all the clubs. There is a 64-degree lob wedge, but 60 degrees is sufficient for most golfers.

HYBRIDS

Hybrids deserve their own section. They are relatively new to the golf world (at least when talking about some game invented hundreds of years ago). Golf club designers recognized that it is not easy to hit an iron out of a heavy rough, and if you can't hit an iron out of it how can you possibly get a wood, with a larger head, through the tall grass? Thus, hybrids were invented. Hybrids are not woods and they are not irons. They are a cross between a wood *and* an iron, giving the club the wood's longer distance with the iron's easier (and shorter) swing. Hybrids are used instead of high-numbered woods and/or low-numbered irons. So you can now have three clubs that can arguably go the same distance but could be played from three different places on a golf course. For example, a 7-wood, 3-iron, and 26-degree hybrid will all go about the same distance, but you would use them at different places on the course. You'd use a 7-wood from the fairway, a 3-iron from the short rough, and a 26-degree hybrid in heavy rough. That is why it is not so easy to have just fourteen clubs in your bag. There are hybrids of 15.5, 16, 18, 21, 22, 24, 26, and 27 degrees; there are fairway woods ranging from 3 to 11 degrees; there are irons ranging from 1 to 10 degrees; and there are drivers ranging from 7 to 12 degrees (and half-degrees in between). Add all of them up and you could have over thirty clubs. Aren't you glad you are limited to fourteen?

Choose your putting weapon.

PUTTER

Yes, the putter is a club and counts as one of the fourteen in your bag. The putter is the most important club in your bag. Why? you may ask. Well, you will probably hit your driver fourteen times a round (presumably, you will not hit your driver on the typically four par-3 holes on a golf course, because they are too short to hit a driver). But I promise you that you will use your putter more than eighteen times a round. If you're lucky, you will use it "only" thirty-five times a round.

Putters are used on the green, although the rules of golf actually allow you to use your putter any time you want. You could actually drive from the tee with your putter, although I wouldn't recommend it. Putters have rules, too. The loft of a putter cannot exceed 10 degrees. Wait a minute. You're telling me that the putter, which simply rolls the ball on the green and hopefully into the hole, has a loft? Actually, yes it does. You may not notice it, but a putter has a loft, often of 5 degrees from truly perpendicular at impact. This helps lift the ball from any indentation it has made.

I should note that most manufacturers produce golf clubs specifically designed for women. The clubs typically have lighter clubheads, higher lofts, and lighter grips and shafts. Likewise, some manufacturers create longer clubs for taller men. I have cut down my putter to 32 inches (the standard is 35) because I am shorter than the average golfer. The point is that as you progress in your golf development you will want to purchase clubs that better suit your size and skill. In fact, all good golf stores will "custom fit" your clubs to your swing. This may cost a little more than an "off the rack" set of clubs, but it is nice to play with a set of clubs specially designed for your swing and game.

Two more club definitions that are solely for the obsessive-compulsive golfer: The "hosel" is the portion of the clubhead to which the shaft attaches. The "ferrule" is the decorative trim ring, usually black, that is found directly on top of the hosel on many woods and irons. And that, my golfing friend, constitutes the golf club.

This is as good a place as any to talk about broken clubs. If a club is broken during play, I have to assume that you didn't break it on purpose (because if you did you shouldn't be playing golf anymore until you get sufficient therapy to address your anger issues). Just in case you have a "friend" who got angry at his 5-iron shot going into the lake and wrapped his club around a tree in response, that club may not be replaced during the round. Period. If, however, a club gets damaged in "the normal course of play" (for example, if your clubhead snaps off your driver when you're making a standard swing), you have the following options: 1) play with the damaged club (this makes for good conversation, but not for good golf); 2) you can repair the club yourself or have someone repair it for you, but you can't delay the game by doing this (so don't plan to run over to your local golf shop to get them to fix it in the middle of your round); 3) replace the club with any other suitable club (so long as it does not delay your round and so long as you do not borrow the club from any other player). You can run to your locker to get that extra driver you stowed in there last winter, you can get a replacement from the pro shop, you can call your sister to come over and give you a replacement club. So long as it does not delay the game and you don't borrow it from another golfer, you are home free.

Also, some of today's drivers have adjustable heads that allow you to adjust the weight of the club or enhance a draw or fade in the ball flight. It's okay to adjust your club any time before or after your round, but never during your round.

Before wrapping up the chapter on golf clubs, let me encourage you to identify and attend a "demo day" at your club or local golf course. Virtually all clubs have such a day, where a variety of golf manufacturers gather to show off their wares and encourage you to buy their latest products. A few caveats: First, try a variety of clubs before deciding that that new TaylorMade driver has your name written all over it. Second, do not feel pressured to buy a club at demo day; this is your opportunity to try out a variety of clubs, and — as is true with all investments (and, yes, at today's cost of golf clubs, they are an investment) — taking a few days to think it over is perfectly acceptable and advisable. You will find that club again if you wait a few days to reflect on your anticipated purchase.

Many people believe that the clubs you find at demo day are made to hit "hotter" (which means faster and longer) than the clubs you will actually buy or receive after your purchase. I have not found this to be the case, but make sure you buy from a reputable manufacturer selling at a reputable club so if you do find a discernible difference between the club you demoed and the club you receive you have someone to complain to about it. A manufacturer is not going to want to bite the hand that feeds it (meaning the course that allows it to demo its clubs on an ongoing basis) and if you do have a problem your local club is probably going to be able to remedy it for you promptly and appropriately. Many manufacturers allow you to return a club, purchased during demo day, for a refund or credit within thirty or sixty days of purchase, no questions asked. This is great for many golfers, because it is not unusual to hit a club like a pro on demo day, only to find that its magic spell fades after the clock strikes midnight.

A JOKE TO TELL WHILE YOU'RE LOOKING FOR YOUR BALL THAT DRIBBLED INTO THE POND.

THE POLICE DISPATCHER NOTIFIED A PATROL OFFICER THAT THERE WAS A REPORTED INCIDENT OF DOMESTIC VIOLENCE ON GRAND AND CENTER STREETS. UPON ARRIVING AT THE HOUSE, OFFICER MCNALLY FOUND NELLIE JOHNSON STANDING OVER HER HUSBAND, FRANK, GOLF CLUB IN HAND. FRANK WAS LYING IN A POOL OF BLOOD.

"MRS. JOHNSON, WHAT HAPPENED?" QUERIED OFFICER MCNALLY.

"GOLF, GOLF, GOLF. THAT'S ALL I EVER HEARD ABOUT FROM FRANK. MORNING, NOON, AND NIGHT. I'M JUST SICK OF IT. I TOLD HIM IF HE MENTIONED GOLF ONE MORE TIME I WOULD PRACTICE GOLF ON HIS HEAD. HE SAID I WAS JUST "TEEING OFF" ON HIM AND THAT DID IT. I TOOK HIS 5-IRON AND JUST STARTING WHACKING HIM."

"HOW MANY TIMES DID YOU HIT HIM, MRS. JOHNSON?" ASKED OFFICER MCNALLY.

MRS. JOHNSON ANSWERED, "FOUR, FIVE, MAYBE SIX TIMES. JUST PUT ME DOWN FOR A FIVE."

Chapter 9

Keep Your Eye on the Ball

GOLF BALLS AND BAGS

Hopefully, you will have a nice big pocket in your golf bag to hold enough of those shiny white spheres destined to hit fairways and hazards. First, the golf balls.

THE GOLF BALL

You may not think there is much more to a golf ball than it being white, having dimples, and easily sailing into the woods. But golf balls have significantly evolved since our seventeenth-century forefathers played with wooden balls. It didn't take long for wooden balls to be replaced by the "featherie" ball. The featherie was a hand-sewn leather pouch stuffed with chicken or goose feathers and coated with paint. You wouldn't want to lose those in the moat, now would you?

Despite the progression of golf equipment decade after decade, the featherie was the standard ball for more than two centuries. And if you think those Titleist Pro V1® (generally considered the best golf ball on the market) or Callaway HX Tour® golf balls are expensive, a single featherie ball would cost the equivalent of $10.00 to $20.00 in the United States today. Now, you definitely don't want to lose many of those in the moat!

Between the featherie ball and today's Nike One Tour® golf ball, the

Reverend Dr. Robert Adams Paterson invented the gutta-percha ball (known as the "guttie") in 1848. The guttie was created from dried sap of a sapodilla tree. But what made this ball significant was the discovery that defects on the guttie from nicks and scrapes, resulting from normal use, provided the ball with a truer flight than a brand new guttie. Thus, the invention of the golf ball dimple. I could do a whole chapter on why there are dimples on today's golf ball. Suffice it to say that most golf balls have 250 to 450 dimples, most brands have an even number of dimples and, for those obsessive-compulsive golfers out there, dimpled balls fly farther due to the combination of the two major aerodynamic forces: lift and drag. For a more detailed explanation, see my high school physics teacher.

The dimples on a golf ball help it to fly straighter.

The twentieth century ushered in the multi-layered golf ball. First we had balls with a solid or liquid-filled core wound with a layer of rubber thread and a thin outer shell. This design was the first that allowed manufacturers to fine-tune the length, spin, and "feel" of the golf ball.

In today's golf world there are two basic types of balls: The less expensive balls that anticipate average golfers not being overly thrilled with their $5.00 investment going into the woods on their opening drive, and the balls designed for scratch golfers and pros who are expected to find most of their shots. The words you will hear when discussing these golf balls are "pieces" and "compression."

Let's start with compression. When a ball is hit by a golf club, it is compressed, deformed, and flattened by the force of impact. Energy is transferred from the club to the ball. When there's less compression at the point of impact, there's more energy transferred to the ball. Thus, a hard core makes it easier for average golfers to hit the ball farther, but the flight of the hard-core golf ball cannot be intentionally shaped as easily. Since average golfers typically don't have a clue as to how to shape the flight of their ball (and shouldn't even try), having a ball that goes a longer distance more easily is a smart idea. So a low-compression ball has a harder core, goes farther, and its flight will not deviate as much as a result of how it is struck.

Getting down to specifics, the compression rating for a low-compression ball is typically 70 or 80 (90 is an average compression – a ball with a rating of 100 should not be in the beginner's or average golfer's bag). Manufacturers used to put the compression rating on the box of balls, but golfers quickly realized that balls designed for women golfers routinely had low-compression ratings. Corporate honchos decided that a big, manly golfer didn't want to hit a lady's ball, so they stopped identifying the compression on the box. As a result, now golfers who think of themselves as Mr. Macho can use low-compression balls and their secret will be safe on the course.

What you now typically see on the box is "long distance and great feel," or "long distance with more spin and control." Try translating that into whether or not the ball is a low-compression ball. The best remedy is to simply ask an experienced clerk at a golf shop what golf balls are good for an average golfer (or for examples of low-compression balls).

Low-compression balls are "two-piece" balls. A two-piece ball has a cover that is very durable and a rubber core that creates the proper weight of the ball. There are two-piece "distance" balls, two-piece low-compression balls, and two-piece "performance" balls. What is the difference among these three balls? Two-piece distance balls have the hardest covers, spin less (which means fewer hooks and slices), and are the cheapest of the lot; two-piece low-compression balls have softer covers, so they go farther if your swing is of moderate speed rather than lightning fast. These balls are of moderate cost; two-piece performance balls have large, "springy" cores, with the thinnest cover of the three types of two-piece balls, so they go farther if hit correctly. These are the most expensive of the two-piece balls. The bottom line regarding which of the three types of two-piece balls are best for you comes down to which ball feels best when struck correctly by your club. I like the low-compression ball because 1) I have a moderate swing, 2) it is in the middle range of expense, and 3) it is a good compromise between the hardest cover and the thinnest cover.

Two-piece distance	Two-piece low-compression	Two-piece performance
Harder cover, lowest spin, "least feel," cheapest cost ($10.00 - $20.00 a dozen). **Examples:** Top Flite XL Pure Distance and Callaway Warbird.	Moderate cover hardness, moderate spin, moderate "feel," medium cost ($15.00 to $25.00 a dozen). **Examples:** Titleist Solo (my preferred golf ball), Precept Lady, and Laddie.	Thinnest cover, springiest core, most "feel," highest cost ($20 to $30 a dozen). **Examples:** Srixon Hi-Spin, Srixon Soft Feel, and Wilson True Velocity.

Do golf ball manufacturers stop there? Of course not. Golfers always believe that if they just buy that new ball their game will miraculously improve. So we now have three-, four-, and even five-piece balls. The three-layer ball has a large inner core surrounded by a casing and a thin, soft cover. A four-piece ball carries this design concept one step further, and consists of a small, softer inner core inside a larger, firmer one, although the casing and cover are similar to those of the three-piece ball. TaylorMade (the company that brought you the first steel-head driver many decades ago) has just come out with the first five-piece ball (the Penta TP®). So what is the advantage of a three-, four-, or five-piece ball over the two-piece ball? The more pieces, the more spin of the ball; the more spin of the ball, the more you can control the shape of the shot or what the ball does when it lands on the green — also, the more room for error if you hit the ball incorrectly. This increased spin is what golfers refer to as "feel": It feels as though they have more control over the ball the softer it feels and the more spin that can be applied. But the trade-off for more feel is less control. Thus, the more inexperienced the golfer, the more the need to "control" the ball. In other words, the two-piece ball is more forgiving if hit badly than a ball with more pieces. And, finally, as would be expected, the more pieces that a ball has, the higher the cost. Leave the high-compression, multi-layered golf balls to the pros. You'll save money and have more control with a low-compression ball.

You can go crazy deciding which golf ball is right for you and trying to decide if one brand is better than another. In addition, golf ball manufacturers create new lines of golf balls as often as a new and improved driver comes out. If you feel that you play better with a certain ball, by all means play with that ball. What is improving your game is your mental confidence — that's just as important as that good luck ball-marker.

If you want to try some of the more expensive multi-layered balls without taking out a second mortgage, there is a huge market of used golf balls to explore. Remember that the $5.00 ball that another player hits in the pond could end up being your $1.00 used golf ball that looks like it just came out of the box. Used golf balls can be purchased at virtually any golf ball outlet and the Internet will give you pages of mail-order sites.

Used golf balls are rated by various grades. A used golf ball in mint condition will have the appearance and feel of a ball that has only been hit once. Imperfections are very minor, if noticeable at all. You will often find corporate, team, personal, or tournament logos in the mix of a bag of mint-condition used golf balls. A rating of AAA means these recycled balls look, feel, and play like new. There just may be some minor surface scratches or imperfections. Balls with a rating of AA will have minor scuffing and their color may not be as bright as mint or grade AAA balls.

Another option you have is to purchase practice balls, which will be clean and playable, but have obvious signs of use. They are great to use to practice chipping in your backyard or to carry in your bag after you have lost a half dozen of your $5.00 balls.

Since my early days of playing golf I have always played with used, low-compression golf balls. On average, they cost me less than $1.00 a piece and, frankly, not only did my game not improve with a $5.00 ball, but I was so concerned about losing the ball that my swing became tentative. Tentative is another word for hitting lousy and losing the ball anyway. I found no difference between a used golf ball in mint condition and a golf ball that was brand new, except for the cost. And I love it when I get a bunch of logo balls in my shipment of used golf balls. This makes it easier for me to recognize and identify my ball on the fairway or green (or in the woods for that matter). What's more, if another playing partner happens to be hitting the same brand golf ball I am, it is fun for me to claim ownership of the one with the Torrey Pines Golf Course logo.

This is a good time to tell you the rule about changing golf balls during a round of golf. Most professional tournaments invoke the "one ball rule," which requires all players to play with only one type of ball during the entire round of golf (meaning if you start your game with the Callaway HX Bite golf ball, you may use only that brand of golf ball throughout the entire round). One good thing about not being a professional is that this rule seldom applies to us. You may play with any ball at any time during your round so long as you change the ball between holes and not during one hole (unless you lose your ball during the hole, of course). So, you can tee off with a Pinnacle Gold Distance golf ball and on the second hole switch to a Precept U-Tri Extra Spin golf ball. Knock yourself out.

THE GOLF BAG

I love my golf bag. It's huge and it holds everything I could possibly want or need on the golf course (or if I was lost in the woods for a couple of years). As a Michigan alumnus, my bag is a bright maize (that's yellow) and blue with MICHIGAN emblazoned across both sides. Have fun with your golf bag and club covers. Make a statement about who you are.

1. Carry bags — The carry bag is the standard golf bag that's meant to be carried over your shoulder. Although it will have storage pockets for tees, balls, etc., it's typically made of lightweight materials and is relatively inexpensive. If you don't mind carrying the weight of your clubs, this is the bag for you.

In recent years, there has been an incredible evolution of carry straps. It used to be that you traditionally just slung the carry golf bag over one shoulder and headed out, hunched over, destined to get tired by the ninth hole. Today, however, most carry bags have a dual shoulder-strap system that balances your clubs so perfectly that you will feel a great weight — literally – has lifted from your shoulders.

The heavier cart bag with its cousin, the lighter stand bag.

2. Cart bags — Cart bags, in contrast to carry bags, are larger, heavier, and meant to be secured to a cart and driven around without being removed from the cart until the end of the round. My Michigan bag is a cart bag (which I could only carry about halfway down the first fairway). I like my cart bag because I want everything I could ever need while playing golf to be in my bag. Most cart bags are equipped with loads of extra storage and, because they are not meant to be carried, they do not have to be made of lightweight material.

3. Stand bags — Stand bags come in either the carry or cart variety, but what makes them unique is that they have fold-out legs that keep the bag upright at a slant (so you don't have to lay it on the ground). Typically, stand bags come as carry bags, because if a cart bag is too heavy the legs aren't going to be able to support its weight.

4. Travel bags — Travel bags are designed for those golfers who hate to rent clubs when they travel. I am one of those golfers, primarily because I am short and rented putters, being of standard length, are far too long for me. I have found two basic types of travel bags: One in which you insert your entire bag (be it a carry or cart bag) into the travel bag, or the other, in which the golf bag is constructed as a self-contained travel bag. A bag in which you insert your own golf bag is typically made of heavy-duty canvas, whereas the travel bag that serves as the golf bag when you get to your destination has a hard-shell case to withstand bumps and bruises.

There are as many varieties of travel bags as there are places you can travel to play golf, so just pick one that fits your temperament. I find the hard-shell case easier to transport, but I tend to travel light with fewer suitcases. If you are going to lug around a lot of pieces of baggage anyway, and you're intent on taking your own bag and clubs, if you use a canvas travel bag for them it will not really add any extra burden to your trip. And the advantage is that you have everything you normally have in your bag on hand wherever you play.

There is no real difference between the golf bags for women and those for men except, as would be expected for women, the bags are more colorful, more stylish, and can even be the product of well-known fashion designers (Christian Audiger, Walter Genuin).

5. Miscellaneous — Some other recent innovations of note: I like the golf bag that has a slot on the outside for your putter, so it doesn't get banged around and you have easy access to it. Also, in the past, golf bags had five or six open sections in which to put your clubs. I like a bag that has a different slot for each club so I can put them in sequence and find them easily (and notice if one is missing). The separation of each club also protects graphite shafts from being scratched. Some golfers with the old bags buy plastic "chutes" in which each club can be slid. This is another "golf nerd" item (remember iron club covers?). I don't use them, but if you like the idea and don't care about being ridiculed by your playing partners, go for it. Some of the newer bags actually have a compartment to keep soft drinks (or harder beverages) cold. I can't wait until the next generation of golf bags have beer on tap!

A JOKE TO TELL WHILE YOU'RE CHANGING YOUR GOLF GLOVE.

TOM'S HANDICAP WAS 14, SO EVERYONE WAS SURPRISED WHEN HE WALKED UP TO THE CLUB PRO, FREDERICK, A SCRATCH GOLFER, AND CHALLENGED HIM TO A MATCH FOR $100.00. RATHER THAN GET STROKES, TOM SAID TO FREDERICK, "I GET TWO 'GOTCHAS' DURING THE ROUND."

"'GOTCHAS?'" FREDERICK RESPONDED. "I'VE NEVER HEARD OF A 'GOTCHA.' WHAT'S THAT?"

TOM SAID, "DON'T WORRY, I'LL USE ONE OF MY 'GOTCHAS' ON THE FIRST TEE AND THEN YOU'LL UNDERSTAND."

FREDERICK FIGURED THAT WHATEVER A "GOTCHA" WAS, GIVING TOM TWO OF THEM WAS NO BIG DEAL, ESPECIALLY IF ONE WAS USED ON THE FIRST TEE. SO HE AGREED TO THE MATCH AND HE AND TOM HEADED OUT TO THE FIRST TEE TO BEGIN THEIR MATCH.

FOUR HOURS LATER, GOLFERS IN THE CLUBHOUSE WERE AMAZED TO SEE FREDERICK HANDING TOM $100.00. WHEN FREDERICK ENTERED THE CLUBHOUSE THEY ASKED HIM WHAT HAPPENED.

"WELL," FREDERICK EXPLAINED, "ON THE FIRST TEE, AS I WAS STARTING MY BACK SWING, TOM KNELT BEHIND ME, REACHED UP BETWEEN MY LEGS, GRABBED MY CROTCH, AND YELLED 'GOTCHA!' HAVE YOU EVER TRIED TO PLAY EIGHTEEN HOLES OF GOLF WAITING FOR THE SECOND 'GOTCHA'?"

Chapter 10

You Can Look Like a Pro Even If You Don't Play Like One

GOLF CLOTHING

While it is true that "clothing makes the man" (and woman), this does not necessarily mean that golf clothes can make you a better golfer. But my philosophy has always been that if you can't play well at least you can *look* as though you do. And just so you know that it is better to learn your lesson from a book rather than on a golf course, let me tell you what happened to me the first year of my golf "development."

I was invited by a friend to play golf at his country club. It was a beautiful Maine summer day — sun shining, blue sky, 80 degrees. So I wore my golf shoes, golf socks, golf shorts, and my favorite Beatles T-shirt. Wrong! T-shirts are a no-no on most golf courses, and certainly on a hoity-toity country club course. To make matters worse, I didn't even notice that no one but me was wearing a T-shirt and my host was too polite to point out my fashion faux pas. But now, years later, when I think back on that day I am still embarrassed. There may be courses that you are allowed to wear T-shirts emblazoned with your favorite rock band. My advice: Don't. Today's golf shirts are so fantastic that you can wear them out to a fancy dinner, let alone to play golf. Most clubs today require a shirt with a collar, so just wear one anytime you play golf and you can't go wrong.

You may notice that golf professionals always wear long pants. This is not because they have knobby knees. It is because it is a requirement of their professional golf association (the PGA). Here is one advantage to not being a pro: You can wear shorts! Actually, the women's professional golf association (LPGA) allows women to wear shorts at their tournaments — another example of when men should follow the lead of their much smarter gender counterpart. But don't wear cut-offs, denim shorts, or gym shorts. Michael Jordan may be a great golfer, but you don't see him wearing his basketball shorts on the golf course now, do you?

If you want to look professional and wear long pants you are more than welcome to do so. However, do not wear jeans when playing golf. Jeans are to your bottom half what T-shirts are to your top half: Not allowed at most good golf courses. Wear collared shirts and normal shorts or regular pants and you will fit right in no matter how bad your game is. As a frivolous tip, if you do prefer long pants, wear a pair that does not have cuffs. Cuffs are destined to trap dirt even if you are lucky enough to avoid the woods and roughs.

The golfer on the right is dressed for success; the golfer on the left is dressed for miniature golf.

Women readers will not be surprised that their golfwear has become tremendously stylish and varied. While men are pretty much stuck with pants or shorts and a golf shirt, clothing designers for women have now produced skirts, capris, culottes, ruched shirts, drop-neck polos — the list is endless. Women can be as stylish on the golf course as they would at a formal dinner! Colorful and even flamboyant outfits may look terrific on women golfers, but male golfers should be cognizant of the "nerd factor." Men, before you go out and buy that bright lime-green shirt, hot pink shorts, and those lovely matching yellow socks, if you are not 100 percent positive that you will be impressing everyone with your game, why call unnecessary attention to yourself? I am all for wearing colorful clothing, but you can dress with power and do so tastefully. That way, if your golf game goes south you'll always be remembered as a golf Beau Brummell.

Also be weather-conscious when you select your clothing for your round of golf. Golf-clothing manufacturers have created ideal materials for playing in all types of weather. The new moisture-wicking materials are designed to keep you cooler in hot weather by transferring moisture away from your body to the outer layer of the fabric. Virtually all good golf-clothing manufacturers are using such advanced fabrics in the production of their golf shirts.

Also, keep in mind the science of heat and color. Back to science class: White reflects, black absorbs. So, if it is a really hot, clear, sunny day and you are wearing black, you are going to absorb a great deal more light from the sun, which will be converted to heat. If you wear white, it will reflect the sunlight away from you. Conversely, if it is a sunny day but chilly, you may want to wear black clothing to absorb more heat. This is why meteorologists are a golfer's most important clothing advisor.

I mentioned golf shoes in an earlier chapter. Wear golf shoes. Golf shoes are spiked (today, virtually all spikes are plastic and no longer steel), so your shoes will grip the ground better as you use all that power to strike the ball. Sneakers can be used in a pinch but, if the ground is wet, rubber sneakers will afford you little stability. I wear golf sneakers when I play in shorts and I wear the more traditional, black oxford golf shoes when I wear pants.
Wear a hat. It can be a baseball hat, a straw hat, or a bonnet (okay, maybe not a bonnet). The point is to cover your head. We older golfing men who believe our hair is not thinning out on the top of our head will get a rude

awakening when that bald spot gets sunburned from being exposed to the sun for five hours. And for you women golfers, I often hear the complaint about having "hat hair" after a round of golf (meaning your beautiful shag cut now looks like a conehead). But don't forget that a hat also keeps the sun out of your eyes and off of your face, preserving that beautiful Oil of Olay skin of yours!

So let's put together your outfit for the day. It is a warm, sunny day, so you opt for shorts. You'll probably want the low cut socks to go with the sneaker golf shoe, a light-colored collared shirt, and a baseball hat with your favorite golf course, sports team, or equipment manufacturer stitched across the front. If it is a cooler day and you opt for long pants, you will wear dark-colored socks with dark-colored oxford golf shoes, a dark-colored collared shirt, and any hat that strikes your fancy. A nice belt, sunglasses if necessary, a sweater if appropriate (either sleeveless or with sleeves, depending on your preference), and you can be a model for any golf magazine. Women, you already know how to dress for every occasion. But be aware that the new golf clothing technology provides clothing that is lightweight, sun protective, and stylish.

So now that you know what to wear, a word about where, when, and how to get into your clothing. It's difficult to change your clothing in your car (and could involve the police if that woman parks next to you right when your knickers are around your knees). Most courses have a locker room. If they don't, use the bathroom. I always bring street shoes with me and change into my golf shoes in the locker room. Not only does that save wear and tear on my golf spikes (and plastic golf spikes wear out very quickly), but I then have street shoes to change back into if my group has a drink after the round (and what group wouldn't do that?).

Since Maine is my home state, I am an expert on cold-weather golf. But even golfers in Miami may find themselves faced with 40-degree weather, sleet, and rain. I have a rain jacket in my golf bag at all times (I told you I have everything I could possibly ever need stored in my golf bag). No jacket is 100 percent waterproof, but the better-quality jackets usually stay driest the longest. Golf manufacturers make golf gloves for cold or wet weather. If it starts to rain and you don't have a rain glove (of course I have a pair in my bag) it is better to take off your glove rather than get it soaking wet. A wet golf glove that is not constructed for rain play will not make it easier to grip your club.

Back to playing in cold weather: Dress in layers. The insulation provided by multi-layering, combined with the body heat generated as you swing your club (many times), will quickly acclimate you to the cooler conditions. It is also easy to take off clothing as the day warms up. Take it from the voice of experience: Playing cold and miserable is, well, cold and miserable. But being warm as toast while playing on a cool, fall foliage day is the next best thing to heaven.

A JOKE TO TELL WHILE YOU'RE REPLACING A DIVOT ON THE FAIRWAY.

JIM WENT GOLFING WITH HIS PAL, EDDIE. WHEN HE ARRIVED HOME TWO HOURS LATER THAN EXPECTED, HIS WIFE, JULIE, ASKED HIM, "WHAT TOOK YOU SO LONG?"

JIM SAID, "HONEY, IT WAS JUST A TERRIBLE DAY. ON THE THIRD HOLE, EDDIE HAD A HEART ATTACK AND DIED RIGHT THERE ON THE FAIRWAY."

JULIE RESPONDED, "OH, SWEETIE, THAT MUST HAVE BEEN JUST HORRIBLE FOR YOU!"

JIM REPLIED, "IT WAS A LIVING HELL. FIFTEEN HOLES OF 'HIT THE BALL, DRAG EDDIE, HIT THE BALL, DRAG EDDIE...'"

Chapter 11

It's Time to Hit the Links: Setting Up Your Golf Game

SELECTING A COURSE TO PLAY

There are three basic types of golf courses you will encounter: Private, public, and municipal. Let's talk about your options.

Private clubs are, well, private. They are country clubs or golf courses reserved for guests of a resort or a hotel. This does not necessarily mean you will never be able to play on them. Many charity golf tournaments, open to the public, are played on private golf courses. If you know a member of a private club who will invite you to play, there's your ticket in. And playing on a private golf course is usually a rare treat because it could easily be the top shelf of golf courses in your area.

A few things to remember: Sometimes the club will allow guests to pay a green fee; sometimes the course will charge all fees to the member and not allow a guest to pay for his play. I don't know of any circumstance in which you should not at least offer to pay your host. Yes, he may say it's on him, but it is unlikely that he would be insulted by you offering. That's far better than looking like a cheapskate and not offering to chip in at all. It's easy to say, "Will the pro shop allow me to pay for my round separately?" or "Please tell me the cost of the round so I can reimburse you." If he refuses your offer, you don't need to make an issue out of it. But it would not be impolite to ask if you can pick up dinner or drinks after the round or the next time you go out.

Remember that you are playing on the course of your host's private club and you are a reflection of him or her. Act as though you were having dinner at your in-law's house (of course, I have to believe playing golf at a country club beats dining with the in-laws). Don't act out, don't drink too much, don't insult the cart driver, don't throw your club. In other words, be on your best behavior. Also, make sure that you ask your host before you get to the club if there is any particular dress code, although if you simply dress as though you were playing in a golf tournament you are unlikely to go wrong (or dress as you would if you were having dinner with your in-laws and you actually *wanted* them to like you). Feel free to ask if there are any customs or practices unique to the club. Is tipping allowed (or expected)? Is the locker room available to guests? Is there a requirement to be at the club a certain amount of time prior to teeing off? In short, it's better to be embarrassed by asking questions of your host rather than to have him or her be embarrassed by you acting inappropriately. Playing on a private course is a treat and a privilege. Behave properly and you will be asked back.

A public golf course is a course available to the public at large. It differs from a municipal course in that a municipal course is owned by a town or city. A public course is owned privately. The vast majority of your rounds will be played on a public course. There are many magazines and Web sites that rate the quality of various private or public golf courses. However, I make it a point to try as many different courses as possible. You may very well find an unknown jewel in the hinterlands. I have played every golf course in Maine within three hours of my home. By happenstance, I discovered the Clinton Golf Course, a small nine-hole golf course run by a local family in Clinton, Maine (a bustling community of 3,500 people), with starting times at intervals of thirty minutes. You will never find this course on any national ranking (and many Mainers are unaware of it), because it is not in the mainstream of public courses. However, it is one of my favorite courses to play and you can find similar special courses in your area by asking golf shops and golf pros, and by surfing the Web.

As stated above, a municipal golf course is a public course owned by a municipality. These courses can be as good as a regular public course — and sometimes they're even better. They can also be a cow pasture. Regardless, because they are typically subsidized by a municipality, the green fee is typically much lower than at a private course and, as a result, the municipal course will usually be much more crowded than other courses. Nonetheless, they can be fun to play and easier to get on than a more "upscale" course.

WHEN JACK NICKLAUS WON THE MASTERS IN 1963, AT THE AGE OF 23, HE BECAME THE YOUNGEST PROFESSIONAL TO WIN THE TOURNAMENT. THEN, IN 1986, HE BECAME THE OLDEST PERSON TO WIN THE MASTERS (AT AGE 46). IN 1997, TIGER WOODS BECAME THE YOUNGEST GOLFER TO WIN THE MASTERS, AT AGE 21.

STARTING TIMES

Virtually all good golf courses require a group to schedule a starting time, which is simply a prearranged time-slot when your group is anticipated to tee off. The busier the day, the more likely the need to reserve a starting time in advance (just as Miami is busier during the winter months, golf courses are typically more crowded on weekends). The interval between starting times will often indicate how crowded a golf course will be. For example, with starting times thirty minutes apart at the Clinton Golf Course, you would not expect to see a lot of golfers in front of you, behind you, or next to you for that matter.

If a golf course schedules starting times every eight minutes, you are likely to bump heads (or balls) with other foursomes. It is always a good idea to schedule a starting time, even if you plan to play on a Tuesday at 11:00 a.m. (when you assume no one else will be playing golf except you). However — and this is one of my major golf pet peeves — if you have scheduled a starting time and then you decide not to play for some reason, call the pro shop back and cancel the starting time. Even if it was a Tuesday, 11:00 a.m. starting time. Do not think it doesn't matter. It does matter. There may be other golfers wanting to play, but unable to schedule a round because your slot is taken. The pro shop will appreciate your making the effort to call to cancel the starting time and golfers on the waiting list will appreciate it even more.

Some courses require a credit card to hold a time slot. You shouldn't be overly timid about providing the course with this security, but just make sure you know how far in advance you must cancel the round without getting charged for not showing up. You can't really blame the course for wanting to charge you if you reserve a time but then bail out without notice, particularly on a busy day when they may have turned away other groups. Just be conscientious and courteous to the club and other players and you will be rewarded next time you want the course to squeeze you in on a busy day.

Many times, particularly if you travel, you need to reserve starting times through an agency. I much prefer to schedule my starting time directly with the pro shop if possible. You don't always know if you are being charged a fee for using an agency and you'll find talking directly with the pro shop gives you more flexibility in planning your round. However, on the tippy-top level of top-shelf golf courses (the Old Course, Torrey Pines, Pinehurst, Pine Valley, etc.) you will not get a starting time without using an agency.

Okay, so you have selected the course on which you are going to play, you have put together your foursome, and the big day is here. What do you do now?

First, is there inclement weather? If it is a cold day, there may be a frost delay. If there is a frost delay, every starting time will be shifted forward. In other words, if you have a 9:00 a.m. starting time and the 8:00 a.m. group was delayed because of frost, your starting time will be affected too. If one is delayed, all are delayed. So if you don't want to sit around the clubhouse for two hours waiting for your starting time, call the pro shop, ask if there is a frost delay, and ask them when you are likely to be able to tee off (if ever). This applies to any weather-related condition that could delay your game (rain, snow, tornadoes, hurricanes, volcanoes).

Also note that, as a standard rule, if there is lightning in the area, play will be suspended (usually by the sounding of a course-wide horn) until thirty minutes have passed without any evidence of lightning.

How early you should get to a golf course depends on your routine practice before teeing off. Are you going to get to the course dressed for golf or are you going to change your clothes in the locker room? Are you going to peruse the merchandise in the pro shop? Are you going to eat lunch before your round begins? How long do you typically take on the range or practice green before you tee off? Here is my standard rule: I allow five minutes to change my clothing, five minutes to sign in at the pro shop (I typically wait until after my round to peruse the merchandise), thirty minutes on the practice range and practice green, ten minutes for hobnobbing — saying "hi" to people I haven't seen in a while, discussing the meaning of life with the greenskeeper — and at least five minutes to be on the first tee waiting for my group to tee off. Throwing in another five minutes for good measure, I plan to be at the golf course an hour before my starting time. That works well for me.

I have playing partners who show up as I am teeing off. I don't particularly like feeling anxious about whether or not they're going to make it, but if it works for them and I choose to play with them, so be it. Also, remember to allow extra time to get to a golf course if it is a distance away from you (and there's unanticipated traffic) or if you are unfamiliar as to where it is located and you are relying on your GPS (just in case you take a left turn into a lake because your GPS told you to).

YALE HAS WON THE MOST NCAA DIVISION I MEN'S TEAM GOLF CHAMPIONSHIPS WITH A TOTAL OF 21 WINS – HOWEVER, THEY HAVE NOT WON A TEAM GOLF CHAMPIONSHIP SINCE 1943. SECOND IS HOUSTON WITH 16 WINS, ALTHOUGH THEIR LAST VICTORY WAS IN 1985.

CHECKING IN

There is never a time you will play golf that you do not check in at the pro shop. Never. Even if you are a guest at a private club, check in with the pro. Many courses have a "starter" on the first tee. This is the man or woman who makes sure everyone in the group has paid their green's fee and that the group is teeing off on time. So when you pay for your round at the pro shop ask the cashier if there is a starter and which slip you need to show him when you get to the first tee. You should also feel free to ask the pro where you go to get your cart, the location of the practice range, the practice green, and the first tee.

The starter will make sure you've paid, and that you tee off on time and have a scorecard.

Although I typically defer checking out the major pro shop merchandise until after my round, there are items you may need prior to playing. Most pro shops will give away ball mark repair tools, plastic ball markers, and tees. If that's not the case at the course you're playing, and you need these items, make a stop at the pro shop and buy them. Some courses sell, or give away, detailed maps of the golf course. These are indispensable if you do not have a GPS or if you have not played on the course before. Since you should already have insect repellent and sunblock in your bag, you shouldn't need to buy them at the pro shop. But if you did not heed my warning and you don't have these items already, buy them there.

PRACTICE RANGE

Most courses have a practice range. The use of a practice range before a round is entirely a personal preference. I spend limited time on the practice range, because I only have about forty good swings a round and I don't want to waste most of them on the range. However, you should feel free to follow your personal pre-game routine in any manner that suits you.

Just make sure you plan in advance how much time you need to prepare for your game so you're not late getting to the first tee. Also, make sure you only practice on the area designated for practice (don't start hitting spare balls out onto the highway to warm up). If the course has roped off a specific area on the practice range for golfers to use that day (the idea being to allow other parts of the range to heal) stay within the designated location.

PRACTICE GREEN

It continues to amaze me how many golfers will devote thirty minutes on a practice range to hitting nothing but their driver and then they'll spend only three minutes on the practice green. This is not a golf instruction book, but simple math dictates that you are going to putt many more times than you are going to drive. So let me share with you my sage advice: Spending as much time on the practice green as you do on the range will pay multiple dividends when you are bending over that three-foot putt to win the hole. Finally, it's a bonus if the course has a practice chipping area or a practice sand trap. All of these practice areas tell you a great deal about the conditions of the course before you start playing.

STRETCHING

Do you want to play golf when you're eighty years old? If so, stretch your body before you begin your game. Even just swinging the driver with a weight attached will make your transition onto the golf course easier and you'll feel more physically healthy. Stretch your legs, stretch your shoulders, rotate your head, do whatever you have to do to feel limber and relaxed. If you pull a muscle on the first tee because you didn't stretch beforehand, all the practice in the world is not going to help you.

TIME TO PLAY

Okay, you're all warmed up, you are dressed properly, you've taken your practice swings, and you're ready to go. Get to the first tee five minutes before your starting time. If the group before you is teeing off don't start washing a dozen golf balls at the tee box while they're hitting. Quietly wait your turn, stay a deferential distance from the group on the tee, and keep your conversation brief and relatively quiet.

A JOKE TO TELL WHILE YOU'RE MARKING YOUR BALL.

TOMMY WAS LOOKING TO MAKE A FAST BUCK ON THE GOLF COURSE WHEN EIGHTY-YEAR-OLD SEYMOUR ARRIVED AT THE CLUBHOUSE. "HEY, PAL," TOMMY SAID TO SEYMOUR. "WOULD YOU LIKE TO PLAY A ROUND WITH ME? AND MAYBE WE CAN MAKE IT MORE INTERESTING BY BETTING $100.00 ON THE ROUND. WHAT DO YOU SAY?"

SEYMOUR AGREED TO THE MATCH AND WHEN TOMMY ASKED HIM HOW MANY STROKES HE NEEDED, SEYMOUR RESPONDED, "OH, I DON'T NEED ANY STROKES. I'M A PRETTY SOLID GOLFER. MY ONLY PROBLEM IS GETTING OUT OF DEEP BUNKERS." SO OFF THEY WENT TO PLAY THEIR MATCH.

TOMMY WAS A DECENT GOLFER, BUT SEYMOUR WAS REALLY GOOD. IF TOMMY DIDN'T HAVE THIRTY YEARS ON SEYMOUR, HE WOULD HAVE BEEN FIVE STROKES DOWN. AS IT WAS, HE WAS BARELY HOLDING HIS OWN.

SEYMOUR EVEN HIT THE BALL OUT OF A COUPLE OF BUNKERS LIKE A PRO. TOMMY THOUGHT TO HIMSELF, "WELL, HE SAID HE HAD TROUBLE GETTING OUT OF DEEP BUNKERS AND THERE ARE A LOT OF THOSE ON THE BACK NINE."

SURE ENOUGH, THEY WERE EVEN WHEN THEY REACHED NUMBER 18 AND SEYMOUR PUT HIS DRIVE RIGHT IN THE MIDDLE OF THE BIG, DEEP BUNKER PROTECTING THE GREEN. "I'VE GOT HIM NOW," TOMMY THOUGHT TO HIMSELF. HOWEVER, AFTER SLIDING DOWN INTO THE BUNKER AND TAKING HIS STANCE OVER THE BALL, SEYMOUR HIT A GREAT SHOT, FLOATING THE BALL UP AND OUT OF THE BUNKER. THE BALL HIT THE FRINGE IN THE PERFECT SPOT, AND ROLLED SIX INCHES FOR AN EASY TAP-IN BIRDIE THAT WOULD WIN THE MATCH.

TOMMY HAD HAD ENOUGH. "YOU SANDBAGGER," TOMMY SNARLED AT SEYMOUR, WHO WAS STILL IN THE BUNKER. "I THOUGHT YOU SAID YOU HAD TROUBLE GETTING OUT OF DEEP BUNKERS!"

"I DO," SEYMOUR RESPONDED. "CAN YOU GIVE ME A HAND OUT OF HERE?"

Chapter 12

Let the Games Begin: The First Tee

It is almost time to hit that first ball. Now that we have prepared to play golf, let's talk about preparation on the first tee. In this section I'll answer such questions as:

- What's in that box on the first tee?
- Where do I hit from?
- Who hits first?
- What's the match?

And a whole lot more.

Okay, let's begin.

THE TEE BOX

The tee box is the area at the beginning of every hole from which the golfers hit their first ball. However, there is not just one set of tees: Golf course architects have designed courses to adjust for different levels of skill by providing different tee boxes.

Golf course designers place hazards and sand traps at strategic locations from each tee box based on the assumption that golfers of a particular level of proficiency will be able to overcome the obstacle in front of them.

However, if you are an average player and you tee off from the hardest tee box, your chance of clearing that hazard (which you would have had a fairly good chance of avoiding had you teed off from an easier tee box) has been considerably reduced.

Some golfers simply believe that golf course architects are sadistic and were placed on earth to torment them. This is true, but that's beside the point: If you play from the tee box designed for your level of play, you will enjoy the game more and have a better chance of avoiding the pitfalls laid out before you.

So how do you know which set of tees is correct for your level of play? The pro shop will tell you which tee box the designer planned for golfers with your handicap or average score. Of course, not everyone you are playing with has the same level of skill. A more experienced golfer may not want to play from the tee designed for the beginning golfer.

But that's okay. Different golfers can hit from different tee boxes. The better golfer can play from the more difficult tee box and then you can move up to your tee box and hit away. However, since human beings — even golfers — have the capacity for compromise, it is not unusual for the group to just agree to a tee box that is acceptable to all of the players, even if each golfer alone would normally hit from a different tee box.

TEE MARKERS

Most courses will have at least three different tee box placements, and many have four or five. There are a few that have six, but they are just showing off. No matter how many tee boxes a course offers the golfer, the one that results in the longest course distance is intended for very low handicappers (typically a handicap of well under 10). The slang word for this tee box is "the tips." Sometimes, if you are just playing for fun (and golf is supposed to be fun, isn't it?), you may want to play a round at your favorite club from the tips. It is fascinating how different a hole can look from each separate tee box. It will also amaze you how much more challenging it is to play from the back tees, and you will have a new appreciation for those who are good enough to play from the tips on a regular basis.

On courses with three tee boxes, the tee box that results in the shortest course distance used to be called the "women's tee." However, not only is that no longer politically correct, but now many women golfers are much better than many men golfers. So this tee box is currently referred to as the "forward tees." Just as no one is required to play from a particular tee, a woman is not required to play from the forward tees. The point of labeling the tees is only to specify which one may be best for each golfer in tournament play.

If there are four tee boxes on a course, the fourth tee box can be for juniors (and would be the box that results in the shortest distance) or for seniors (which would be between the forward tees and the men's tees). There is no set rule for when a player is a junior or senior golfer and, once again, no one is required to play from this tee box. This is simply the tee from which a junior or senior may play in a tournament. At some clubs, if an individual's combined age and handicap is 90 or more (some clubs use 80 and some clubs use 100 as the benchmark), they are considered a senior player. Likewise, at some clubs if an individual is under the age of eighteen, they are considered a junior.

How your score affects your handicap will also be dependent upon what tee you play from. In other words, a higher score from a more difficult tee

Let the games begin.

may have the same effect on your handicap as a lower score from an easier tee. This is explained in greater detail in chapter fifteen.

Every tee box has two markers between which you are required to tee up and hit your ball. Every course identifies each tee box differently and often in very creative ways. It is most common to have each tee box distinguished by a different color: The tips are often black, the second tees blue, and the third tees red. If the course has more than four tee boxes, the additional colors may be white, green, or silver. There is no rule requiring that a particular tee box be a particular color. The markers can be of various shapes and can be items instead of colors: Wood, rocks, flowers, cacti, square, round, long, short — whatever creative markers the pro shop devises.

CHANGING TEES

The rules require you to play from the tee box you started from in tournament play or for your score to count towards your handicap calculations. However, if you start playing from one tee box and then you find the course is playing too easy or too hard, you can certainly change tee boxes if to do otherwise would make your day miserable.

TREATS ON THE TEE BOX

The first tee box can be chock full of nifty items. Since you may have forgotten to get a scorecard from the pro shop, there will likely be a box with scorecards and pencils on the first and sometimes the second tee. The first tee will also often have tees, ball markers, and ball mark repair tools available for your use.

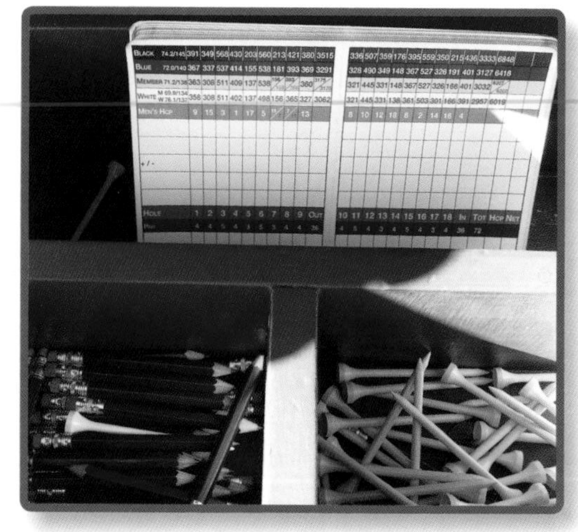

Pick up a tee, a pencil, or a scorecard on the first tee box if needed.

Tee boxes throughout the course will generally have golf ball washers to keep your golf balls nice, shiny, and dirt-free. (Typically, a washer is a metal container on the top of a pole with a handle that pulls up; you put your ball in the hole and move the handle up and down while the bristles inside the container clean your ball). Most tee boxes have a container with a sand and seed mixture. So, if you take out a piece of sod from the tee box on your drive, you can fill the divot with the sand/seed mixture and hasten its repair. This is particularly true on par-3 holes, where more golfers hit irons rather than woods (a wood is not supposed to cause a divot and an iron is). But any time you cause a divot or see one — on the tee box or on the fairway — and you have a sand/seed mixture available (many riding carts have containers with such mixtures right on them), you should fill the divot with the mixture. We'll talk about repairing marks on the green later, but the sand/seed mixture is not used to repair a mark on the green. Usually, you will find a water fountain or water barrel on tee boxes located at various intervals throughout the course. Every course is different, but it is always an adventure to see what goodies the course provides to you on a tee box.

TEE BOX MARKERS

Most tee boxes have a marker showing you the distance to the middle of the green. This is more important information on a par 3 than a par 4 or 5, because, presumably, you intend to have your drive land on the green on a par 3. But if nothing else, it tells you the length of this particular hole.

SCORECARD

Yes, a scorecard is helpful to keep score of your game. You should try to remember to pick up a scorecard in the pro shop when you check in. Likewise, you need a pencil to keep a score (and don't worry if the pencil doesn't have an eraser — it eliminates the temptation of changing your score later in the round). I actually keep in my bag two or three blank scorecards of courses I play regularly, just in case I forget to pick one up in the pro shop or there are none available on the tee. Many courses will have a scorecard on every riding cart.

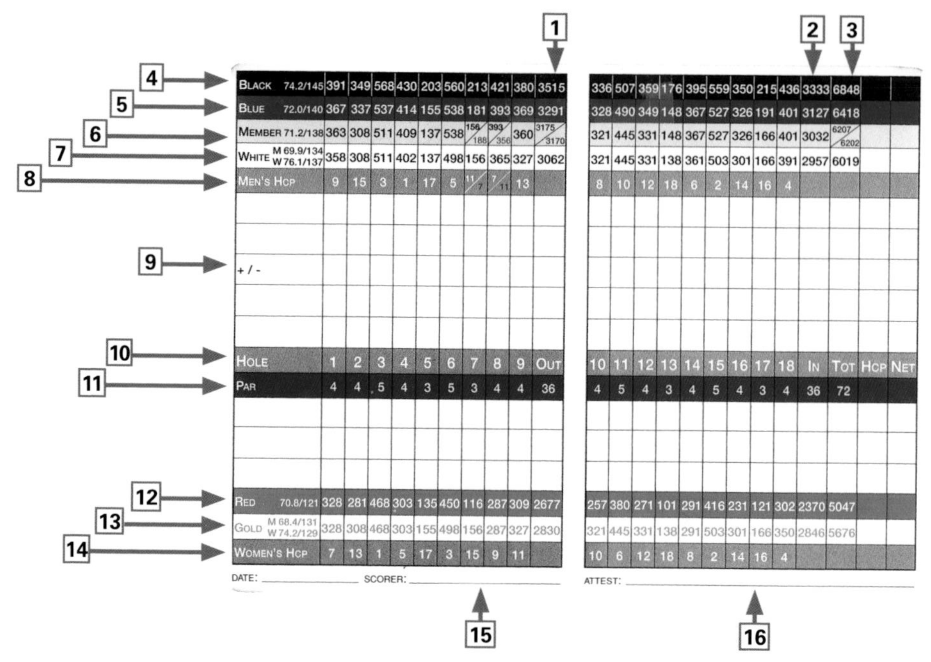

Hole	1	2	3	4	5	6	7	8	9	Out
Black 74.2/145	391	349	568	430	203	560	213	421	380	3515
Blue 72.0/140	367	337	537	414	155	538	181	393	369	3291
Member 71.2/138	363	308	511	409	137	538	156/188	393/356	360	3175/3170
White M 69.9/134 W 76.1/137	358	308	511	402	137	498	156	365	327	3062
Men's Hcp	9	15	3	1	17	5	11/7	7/11	13	
+/-										
Par	4	4	5	4	3	5	3	4	4	36
Red 70.8/121	328	281	468	303	135	450	116	287	309	2677
Gold M 68.4/131 W 74.2/129	328	308	468	303	155	498	156	287	327	2830
Women's Hcp	7	13	1	5	17	3	15	9	11	

DATE: ______ SCORER: ______

10	11	12	13	14	15	16	17	18	In	Tot	Hcp	Net
336	507	359	176	395	559	350	215	436	3333	6848		
328	490	349	148	367	527	326	191	401	3127	6418		
321	445	331	148	367	527	326	166	401	3032	6207/6202		
321	445	331	138	361	503	301	166	391	2957	6019		
8	10	12	18	6	2	14	16	4				
4	5	4	3	4	5	4	3	4	36	72		
257	380	271	101	291	416	231	121	302	2370	5047		
321	445	331	138	291	503	301	166	350	2846	5676		
10	6	12	18	8	2	14	16	4				

ATTEST: ______

The scorecard is the road map to the golf course.

1) Length of front nine from each tee box	**9)** Line to score each hole in match
2) Length of back nine from each tee box	**10)** Hole number
3) Length of whole course from each tee box	**11)** Par for hole
4) Rating & slope from tips	**12)** Rating & slope for forward tees
5) Rating & slope from 2nd tee	**13)** Rating & slope for back forward tees
6) Rating & slope from member tee	**14)** Hole handicap for women
7) Rating & slope from 3rd tee	**15)** To sign in tournament
8) Hole handicap for men	**16)** To witness in tournament

There is a ton of information you can get from a scorecard. It routinely has the distance from the various tee boxes to assist you in deciding which one you want to play. The card will typically have a line or column for up to six players, although do not take this as encouragement to play in any group larger than four. There will also be a line on which, if you are playing a match, you can note if your team won or lost a hole. This line usually has a "+/-" on it. If you and your partner win the first hole, you would put "+1" in this box in the column for the first hole. If you tie the next hole (typically referred to as "no blood") you would either put a "-" in the second column or carry over the "+1." If you lose the third hole (your game is going in the wrong direction) you would either put a "-1" in the third column or put a "0," showing you are even after three holes. And that's the basic system. It's good to see a lot of pluses, but sometimes you win, sometimes you lose.

Often the scorecard will show you a little sketch of the hole so that you can see, in miniature form, if there are any obvious hazards (usually water) or if the hole has a significant dogleg left or right.

The scorecard will also tell you the "slope" and "rating" of the course, based on the tee from which you are playing (these terms will be explained in detail later). In addition, the scorecard will tell you what the "par" is for each hole. Par is the expected number of strokes an expert golfer would need to make to complete a hole. All eighteen holes have an individual par and when these eighteen pars are added up they total "par for the course."

PAR FOR THE COURSE

There are typically two par 3s, two par 5s, and five par 4s on each nine holes of a golf course. This is not mandatory, just average. Thus, the par for nine holes is 36 and the par for eighteen holes is 72. A course may only have one par 5 or three par 3s on a particular nine holes of the course. It doesn't really matter to the golfer, although it could affect the rating of the course since par 5s are typically considered more difficult than par 3s. If a course has more par 3s and fewer par 5s it may indicate an easier golf course and thus a lower rating.

HOLE HANDICAP

The scorecard will identify the handicap of the hole. This is critical information if you are playing a match or a tournament. Most importantly, note that the handicap of each hole on the course is not the same thing as a golfer's individual handicap, although they are like first cousins. Each golfer's individual handicap indicates how his or her expected playing skill compares with that of other players, while the handicap of the hole represents the difficulty of that hole compared to other holes on the course.

The handicap of the hole is a pretty basic concept: The lower the handicap number, the harder the hole. Most of the time handicaps on the front nine will be odd numbers and handicaps on the back nine will be even numbers. So if you are playing the front nine, the hole that has a handicap of 1 is the hardest hole on the front nine. The hole that has a handicap of 17 is the easiest hole on the front nine. Don't let it bother you if you have your worst score on the easiest hole on the course. It happens all the time. The ease of a hole is meaningless if your drive goes out of bounds. Also note that the second hardest hole on the front nine (the three handicap) may actually be harder than the hardest hole on the back nine (the two handicap). That is because the holes on the front nine are compared to each other, not to the holes on the back nine. Also, you may think that the par-5 holes are always harder, thus lower handicapped holes, than par-3 or par-4 holes. Not so. Typically, the hardest holes are the longer par 4s. Rarely is a par 3 one of the toughest holes.

MATCHES

I will go over the most common matches later in the book, but if you are going to play a match, you have to decide to do so and agree on what kind of match to play, as well as form teams, before the first golfer tees off. Let me preface this topic by reminding you that human beings (which may include golfers) have free will and do not *have* to play a match if they don't want to. I am talking about you. Do not be intimidated into playing a match if it makes the game less fun for you. And don't guilt another golfer into playing a match if they don't want to.

Most golfers feel that playing a match makes the game more fun, challenging, and causes a golfer to play better (or at least pay more attention to his or her game). Also, most games are played for very low stakes, although I have seen golfers never speak to each other again over the net loss of one quarter. There is a natural tendency when playing a match to want your team to do better than the other team, which inherently means you want the other team to do worse than your team. When I find myself wanting a friend, who happens to be on the other team, to miss a putt, the game has become too serious for me. That's when I take a vacation from playing matches for a while, or decide not to play a match if there's the possibility that I will be playing against a close friend. You can do likewise. And the other golfers in your group can play a match without you. There are matches for two players, three players, or four players.

All that being said, if you wish to play a match or just go along with the gang, have at it. Just make sure you know what the stakes are, what the rules are, and that you are not playing with other golfers who are so serious that you will need your driver to defend yourself after the round.

MARKING YOUR BALL

We're not quite ready to hit that first ball yet. You have a scorecard and you have enough golf balls and tees. Now, do one more thing that could avoid major headaches later in the round: Mark your golf ball.
This is a basic, but fundamental, necessity of golf: You mark your ball to make sure you can distinguish it from that of any other golfer on the golf course. It is easy to mark your ball: There are all sorts of felt-tip pens available from your local golf store or pro shop. You can mark it any way you wish: Three dots, a smiley face, a tongue sticking out at you. You can't attach a foreign object to the ball, but you can mark it in any manner that will allow you to identify it among others being played by your teammates or any other golfer on the course who may have hit a wayward shot onto your fairway.

Mark your ball in any manner that makes it easily recognizable to you.

Although you are not legally required to mark your ball — even though I strongly encourage you to do so — the bottom line is that you have to be able to distinguish it from any other golfer's ball on the course. Don't assume your teammates are playing with a different brand of golf ball. Before the first ball is hit, you need to know the make of your ball and the number on it. You should also ask the golfers in your group for the same information about their golf balls. If someone is playing the same make and number as you, one of you should switch balls in the event that both of you do not put a distinguishing mark on your respective golf balls.

The reason why marking the ball is better than simply remembering the make and number is that a player on the adjoining hole may hit a ball onto your fairway and you may not know which ball belongs to which golfer. Believe it or not this is fairly common. I love playing with logo balls because it is a very easy way to identify my ball. However, if I'm in a tournament and I'm playing with the same brand of golf ball that was given to everyone else in the tourney by a sponsor, you had better believe that I mark my ball in some distinctive way.

ORDER OF HITTING

Okay, now can we *finally* hit the damn ball? You are on the first tee. Who hits first? In a professional golf tournament, a draw is used to determine who plays with whom in (usually in the first two rounds) and at what time each group tees off. However, we are not going to stand on the first tee and put all of our names in a hat and select an order of teeing off on the first hole. In a very formal match (such as club championship) this would be appropriate (unless the club determines that the lowest-handicapped player should tee off first). If you are playing an informal match, just flip a coin or a tee to determine which team hits first. The order of hitting within the team is completely up to the team. As you will read shortly in the section on "ready play," if no match is being played, then the first one ready to go should get up there and hit away.

NERVES

Okay, you're almost ready to hit your first shot of the day. Let me just tell you one more tiny little secret before you take your first swing: Every golfer is nervous when they are about to hit their opening shot. Every golfer. Without exception. You, me, and every golf pro with whom I have ever spoken. It is universal. It is normal. So just accept it and go with the flow. Since this book is not about golf techniques, I will only give you the one hint I have been told countless times by countless golf pros: Stick to your routine, don't think about your first swing, do the best you can, and have a good time. The rest will work itself out.

TEES ON THE TEE BOX

The tee box is the only place on the course where a tee can be used to (hopefully) help you hit your ball. You don't have to put your ball on a tee, but it is the only place you are entitled to do so. Do not put your ball on a tee on your second shot from the fairway. Do not put your ball on a tee from the hazard. Do not put your ball on a tee on the green. Got it? You are not allowed to put your ball on a tee anywhere other than your drive off the tee box.

Always tee your ball between and behind the imaginary line formed by the two tee markers.

Your ball has to be teed up between and behind the two markers set up on your tee box. If you draw an imaginary line between the two markers you cannot tee up your ball in front of that line. Please reread the last line: You can never — never, never, never — tee your ball in front of the imaginary line drawn between two markers. To do so is a penalty. It is also embarrassing. Golfing buddies just can't wait to tell you that you just hit your ball from in front of the tee markers. In match play, you don't get penalized, but your opponent can make you replay your drive (after snickering at you). In stroke play, it is a two-stroke penalty and you must take your shot over again (and the snickering is optional).

By the way, your feet do not have to be between the two markers when you hit your ball. For example, if you are right-handed and you tee your ball a foot to the right of the left tee marker, your feet can (and will have to) be on the left side of that marker (obviously then, they will not be between the two markers). So long as the ball is between the two markers and behind the imaginary line it doesn't matter where your feet are.

As an aside, you are legally entitled to tee your ball up to two club-lengths behind that imaginary line between the two markers. I've never seen anyone actually measure two club-lengths, but that's the rule in case anyone ever challenges you on your ball placement.

WHERE TO STAND

Believe it or not, this is often the most overlooked rule of etiquette in golf. Some golfers hit a ball just fine despite a distraction. In fact, some golfers need distractions to be able to hit a golf ball! (I routinely talk in the middle of my own back swing.) But if a golfer has a bad shot and you did anything that could be described as a distraction, I guarantee you he will blame you for ruining his shot.

So the first rule of tee-box etiquette is that it is fine to chat when you get to the tee box (so long as there is not another team on the tee box waiting to hit). But when someone is preparing to hit from your group, all talking should end. And that is not just when your teammate swings the club: It is when he is going through his pre-shot routine as well. A good rule of thumb is that when the golfer is teeing the ball up for a drive, that's a good time to wind down conversation and movement.

If you are going to stand on the tee box when someone else is hitting (which is often a good idea because it is also proper etiquette to watch where the ball is going while the golfer's head is down), I recommend standing at a 45-degree angle to the side and behind the golfer, so you're within his range of visibility, but not parallel to him. First and foremost, stand far enough back so he can freely swing a practice swing and his actual drive without the club coming within a mile of your head.

I like the "45-degree" guideline for several reasons. If a golfer cannot see you, he can be distracted by "sensing" you. While you're waiting to hit, it may be hard for you to stand absolutely still and not make any sound. So the golfer about to hit can sense your presence by your breathing, your rustling of clothing, or your just plain fidgeting. His attention could also be diverted if he's worried that you may be close enough to him to get hit. So being out of his sight completely can in itself be distracting (see "getting blamed" above). If you are behind, but within the peripheral view of the hitter, he can see you but you are not such a strong presence as to disturb his concentration. Being parallel to him is too distracting. Standing behind him makes you too invisible. Forty-five degrees is just right. Second (and also important), stand *still.* Don't swing your club. Don't pull the Velcro® on your golf glove. Don't put clubs into or take them out of your bag. Try not to swat mosquitoes. Don't let your shadow extend into his line of sight. Get the point? Just be quiet and watch his ball.

After you have hit your drive, don't be so self-absorbed that you forget that someone is hitting after you. Don't go off to the side and do some practice swings to try to figure out why you duck-hooked your drive into the woods. No one wants to hear a self-diagnosis about your bad shot. We have enough to worry about our upcoming shot without inheriting your negative thoughts about your swing. Either stand to the side and back while the other golfer swings, or return to your cart prepared to move out when the last golfer has hit.

Returning to your cart doesn't mean you should slam your golf club in the bag, zip one of the pockets to get another ball, or curse your bad fortune of having that mosquito bite you right when you were swinging. Your turn is over; it is another golfer's turn. Be as courteous to him as he was to you (or as he *should* have been to you). Remember the "do unto others" adage? It applies to golfers too.

It's okay to sit in the cart while others are hitting. But remember that 1) you won't be in a great position to watch their ball, which is really not very nice since they went out of the way to watch yours, and 2) depending on where the cart is, your presence can be distracting. If the cart is behind and to the side of the hitter, great. If not, make sure to stand in a place that won't distract the golfer and all will be fine.

BALL WASHING

Ball washers are typically found on most tees. This is good. A clean ball goes farther. It bounces better. It looks nicer. But don't start washing all of your golf balls while someone else is hitting his ball. This is more distracting than cursing about that mosquito. Also, only use the ball washer to clean your ball. Licking your ball may be good for the ball, but bad for your health. Fairways have insecticides, pesticides, and fertilizer on them. The ball rolls on all that. Not tasty or healthy.

A JOKE TO TELL WHILE YOU'RE CLEANING WET GRASS OFF YOUR SPIKES.

JOHN WAS A VERY SERIOUS GOLFER. NOTHING COULD GRAB HIS ATTENTION AWAY FROM HIS NEXT HOLE. SO YOU CAN IMAGINE THE AMAZEMENT OF HIS PARTNERS WHEN, PRIOR TO PUTTING ON THE SEVENTEENTH GREEN, JOHN TOOK OFF HIS HAT, PUT HIS PUTTER BY HIS SIDE, AND WAITED UNTIL THE FUNERAL PROCESSION PASSED BY THE GOLF COURSE BEFORE LINING UP HIS PUTT.

"JOHN, THAT'S AMAZING," SAID HIS PARTNER, HENRY. "I HAVE NEVER SEEN YOU GET DISTRACTED FROM YOUR GAME BY ANYTHING, LET ALONE A FUNERAL PROCESSION."

JOHN REPLIED, "WELL, AFTER ALL, I WAS MARRIED TO HER FOR THIRTY-SIX YEARS."

Chapter 13

The Path to Heaven: The Fairway

ORDER OF HITTING ON THE FAIRWAY

Your group has teed off and now you're on your way down the fairway. Who gets to be first to take the next shot? The conventional rule is that after the first shot on the first tee — for every other shot for the rest of the hole — the player who is farthest from the hole hits his ball first. That rule applies every time and for any reason. If you follow this rule, you can never go wrong and never be accused of being rude or impolite.

However, try not to get carried away by this rule. You don't have to measure the distance from the pin with a slide rule to ascertain who is actually farthest from the hole. More importantly, in recent years, with golf becoming so popular and golf courses so congested, the concept of "ready golf" has become the motto of the game. Ready golf means that if you are ready to hit and the person who is supposed to be hitting before you is not, then you *can* and *should* go ahead and hit your ball.

Of course, you should also use your common sense for this rule as well. If your ball is ten feet directly in front of another player, the fact that you can get to your ball a minute before the other player gets to his doesn't entitle you to go ahead and hit your ball first. If you go in front of the other player and hit first, you could potentially slow him down and, thus, slow down the entire group. If you have to wait a minute to hit because the player behind you is trying to decide what club to use, take a moment to look around you and enjoy the scenery. After all, you are here to have fun, aren't you? But if the other player is minutes away from getting to his ball (let's say he's spending time helping another player look for his ball), and you can safely hit your ball and move out of the way before he arrives to hit his ball, which is behind you, then ready play is the way to go.

PACE OF PLAY

The corollary to ready golf is pace of play. Each course has a pace of play that is dependent upon many factors. How busy is the course that day? (Sunny days and weekends make the course more congested.) How difficult is the course? (A difficult course means more lost balls, which means more time to look for lost balls, which means a slower pace of play.) There is no written rule that says a round of golf on a particular course has to be played in a certain number of hours. A rule of thumb is that most courses like to see a round of golf take no more than four hours and fifteen minutes. But on a sunny Sunday, it could turn out to be much longer. Ready golf simply means you should keep up with the pace of play, staying behind the group in front of you and staying ahead of the group behind you. This does not mean you can't take a minute to determine how far you are from the pin or what club to use. However, you should be aware of the flow of the game on that course and on that day. Think of it as being similar to a highway: If every car is going forty-five miles an hour, you should drive a similar speed; if everyone is going sixty-five, you should keep up with the pace of the driving. Same with golf: Keep up with the pace of play.

PICKING UP

All beginning golfers believe that playing with experienced golfers will be a bad experience (for both of them). They're concerned that they'll slow the play down, that the better golfer will be irritated at their poor play, and that, in general, they'll embarrass themselves. Believe it or not, most golfers are so consumed with their own game they have very little awareness of what is going on with your game. But if you play ready golf and keep up with the pace of play, no matter how high your score may be, you will be invited back to play another day.

This may mean that on a particular hole you need to pick up your ball and not finish the hole. *What? You mean to tell me that there are times I should just put my ball in my pocket, and let the rest of the group finish the hole without me?* Yes. Good golfers don't care how well you play, they care how fast you play. So long as you don't unreasonably hold up the pace of play, your skill of play is truly unimportant to the average polite and considerate golf partner (and you don't want to play golf with any other kind of golfer now, do you?).

Now before you worry about the legitimacy of your score if you pick up your ball and don't finish a particular hole, let me put your fevered mind at ease. Depending on what your handicap is, you are only allowed to take a certain number of strokes on every hole anyway. If your score on the hole on which you pick up your ball exceeds the maximum number of strokes you can count on a hole of that par, your actual score is irrelevant. So it is also irrelevant if you finish the hole. In other words, if, based on your handicap, you are not allowed more than eight strokes on a par 5, you are going to get an 8 on that hole whether you picked up your ball after going out of bounds twice and losing your ball three times (meaning you are already lying 10 and you probably should have picked up your ball long before then) or you actually got an 8 for the hole. It doesn't cost you anything to pick up your ball and you avoid slowing down the pace of play. You simply put an "X" for the hole and the pro shop will adjust it for your handicap when you turn in your scorecard (or you can adjust it yourself after your round if you post your own scores).

You should pick up your ball any time you feel that you are slowing down the pace of play and it is clear to you that your play on that hole is probably not going to get a whole lot better (as your anxiety builds, you try to correct what you're doing wrong, but you don't know what you're doing wrong. . . you've been there, you know what I'm talking about). By picking up your ball it will give you some time to calm yourself down and clear your head before the next hole. A new golfer who knows when it is time to pick up his ball and end the torture of a particular hole is always an appreciated teammate. When you reach the green and someone asks you where your ball is, you can simply say, "I'm in my pocket." That means you were wise enough to figure out that this hole just wasn't working out for you and, rather than slow down the pace of play, you picked up the ball and enjoyed the play of others in your group.

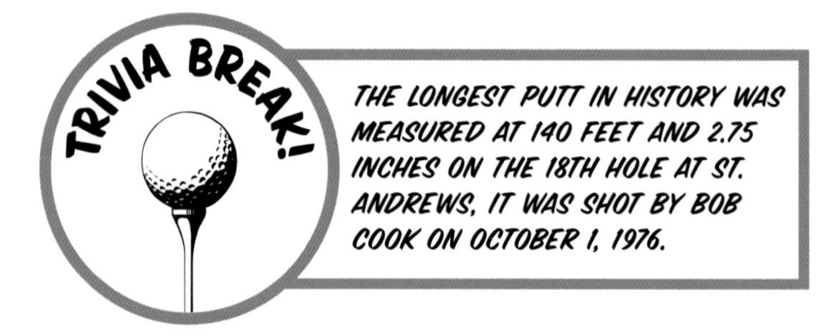

PLAYING THROUGH

If, for some bizarre reason, your teammates have not read this chapter and your group is playing particularly slowly, it's likely that the team behind you will eventually catch up with you and start breathing down your necks.

This does not mean you have to stop playing. If you find your group simply unable to keep pace with the current flow of the course, all you need to do is let the group behind you "play through" (as we discussed in chapter four, this is one of the basic rules of etiquette). How do you know if your group is playing slowly? Well, if the group in front of you is consistently a full hole ahead of you, that probably means you are lagging behind. In fact, my standard rule is that if I am on the tee box of a hole and the next group is already on their tee box on the next hole, my group is probably not keeping up with the pace of play. We need to speed our game up or get out of the way. And that means letting the group behind us play through.

This is easy to do: Wave, whistle, or otherwise signal that they may play through. They will know what you are inviting them to do. That's why they have been glaring at you for the last half hour. As you let them proceed, just make sure to stand far enough to the side (preferably behind a tree) to ensure that an errant shot from their group will not hit you.

Often, particularly if you are almost done with the hole, invite them to play through on the next tee. When you get to it, go ahead and hit your drives, but just wait until they get to the tee box you are standing on, hit their own balls, and are far enough ahead of you so that you can safely play. This is another reason to mark your ball — you may now have eight balls on the fairway and duplication is likely.

It is also perfectly appropriate to allow a single golfer, a twosome, or even a threesome, to play through even if you are keeping up with the pace of play. Don't penalize a golfer for not being able to find enough friends to play a round of golf with. Golf is fun. Waiting forever to hit your next shot is not fun. Anytime there is a space between your group and the group ahead of you, and the players behind you have been on your heels for a hole or two, let them play through.

RANGERS

Just because you are willing to let lots of groups play through does not mean you should feel free to play as slowly as you wish. Many courses have rangers who will drive around and ensure that the pace of play is maintained by all groups. If a course is starting off groups every six to eight minutes, a slow group on the fifth hole will slow down the entire course in a kind of domino effect.

Typically, a ranger may come by and just give you a warning to pick up your pace of play. If he comes around again and there is still no other group in sight in front of you, a ranger can — and will — require your team to pick up your balls and move to the next tee without finishing the hole. You don't want that to happen. That is embarrassing. You can avoid that. Play ready golf. Don't look for that lost ball for ten minutes. Don't spend five minutes on a forty-foot putt that even Lee Trevino can't make.

PLAYING THROUGH OTHERS

Hopefully, your team will be the one that is keeping up with the pace of play and, if anything, you're breathing down the necks of the team in front of you. What do you do if they will not let you play through? Well, first, what you should *not* do is hit a ball that you believe will reach a golfer in front of you. Is the group in front of you being rude by not letting you play through? Of course. But just because they're being rude to you doesn't justify your being rude or, worse yet, a danger to them.

If there is a ranger on the course, next time he comes by feel free to mention to him that the group in front of you is playing obnoxiously slowly. If he is doing his job he will "encourage" them to speed up. Keep in mind that you probably can't see two or three holes in front of you. It may be that they are being slowed down by a group five holes in front of them. The group in front of you is only responsible for playing slowly if there is an open hole in front of them.

And if you are playing as a single, double, or threesome, and the group in front of you is keeping up with the pace of play, there may not be anywhere for you to go even if they let you play through, because the course is just crowded and the pace of play is more like cars stuck on the highway in bumper-to-bumper traffic. Enjoy the fact that you are on the golf course and not in your office and take the extra time to meditate on the beauty of your surroundings.

I will confess that I have little patience for slow play. I have called the pro shop from my cell (the only time I use a cell phone on the golf course) and complained about a slow group that should, but won't, let us play through. I will further confess that one time, after following a particularly slow foursome for five holes when there wasn't another group in front of them for miles, I drove my cart down to the green and asked them, relatively politely, to allow us to play through. They relented (grudgingly) and, fortunately, my entire group had stellar drives. Whew! It would have been embarrassing if all of us had put our drives in the hazard. The point is to not be the group that is so self-absorbed that you don't recognize how you are affecting groups behind you. If you are in front of me, I will come down and remind you.

DISTANCE TO THE PIN

Back to playing golf. Some golfers select what club to play based on how far they are from the hole, since they know they can hit a 3-iron 180 yards or a pitching wedge 110. So it is helpful, if not imperative, to know how distances are marked on the course you are playing. (By the way, I should also mention that the rules of golf state that it is illegal to ask another player what club they think you should hit or what club they are using on a particular shot. But in friendly play, this rule is rarely enforced.)

Virtually all golf courses have markers indicating when you are 100, 150 or 200 yards from the hole. Some will even have 250-yard markers on par-5 holes. These measurements are from the marker to the center of the green.

Some golf courses use landmarks to denote distances. I have played on courses that have little pine trees at the 150-yard mark. I have seen birdhouses erected at the 100-yard mark. The point is that you need to ascertain how distances are marked on the course you are playing. The starter may give you this information before you head out or you can simply ask the pro shop.

The vast majority of courses also utilize sprinkler heads to note distances from that point to the middle of the green (some actually tell you the distance from the front, back, and middle of the green). So if you notice a sprinkler head as you are walking down the fairway toward your ball, see if it has the distance on it.

If your ball is right behind a distance marker and it is impossible for you to hit it because of the marker, you can move the marker (not your ball). If the marker cannot be moved, it becomes "fixed" and you're out of luck. You can't move the marker or your ball. It can become an unplayable lie, but, as described below, that will cost you a stroke. A yardage marker or a hazard stake that can be moved (just as if it was a trash can in your way) are considered movable obstructions and can be moved without penalty. However, you cannot move a tee marker on a tee box and you cannot move an out-of-bounds stake. Why can you move a hazard stake and not an out of bounds stake? Because you can hit your ball from a hazard (hopefully), but you can never hit a ball from out of bounds.

Well, it's great knowing the distance to the middle of the pin, but what if the pin is not in the middle of the green? The greenskeeper will change the location of the pin, often on a daily basis. No, this is not just to torment you (although they do delight in doing that). By changing the location of the pin regularly, they prevent unnecessary wear and tear around one stationary hole. There are various methods that golf courses use to let you know the placement of a hole.

Often, a course will use flag colors to signal the location of the hole on the green. For example, a red flag may represent placement of the hole in the front of the green, white in the middle, and black in the back. If a course is using a flag color-code system, it should be noted on the golf scorecard.

The little flag right below the big flag means the hole is at the back of the green.

Another method that's used is a smaller flag or a plastic ball on the flagpole itself. If the ball is high up on the flagpole, this signals that the hole is towards the back of the green; if it's in the middle of the flagpole, it means the middle of the green, and if it's low on the flagpole it indicates the front of the green. The logic is that if the ball is lower on the pole you could only see it when you're closer to the front of the green.

A third method is a chart that the pro shop provides that shows the greens divided into three to five sections, each with a number on it, and the course having one number denoting the flag placement on all the greens for that day. So, for example, the pro shop will tell you that today the flag placement is number two, meaning that if you look at the chart, wherever section two is, that's where you'll find the flag. It may be back left, or front middle, or middle right. The point is you are told where the flag is on every green for that day. Typically, the chart will be on the riding cart or the scorecard.

Some charts will even note the distance from the back or front edge of the green to the center, so you can become even more obsessive about the precise location of the flag. For instance, let's say the flag placement that day is two and on the chart you see that section two is the back left part of the green. The chart may have a line from the middle to the back with the notation +15. That means it is an additional fifteen yards from the center of the green to the back of the green, so you will have about half that distance (seven or eight yards) to the center of the pin. Simple, huh?

GPS

As we've already discussed, the new GPS technology invented for driving a car was readily adaptable to driving a golf ball. If you are a "distance player," meaning you know how far you hit each club, then it's vital for you to have an accurate prediction of distance to be able to make better club selections. In this case, an investment in a GPS device will pay huge dividends.

I will note that as much as I love my Apple iPhone, I have yet to find an application that comes close to a high-priced GPS or rangefinder. Although there are nifty applications for keeping score and telling me how many times I 3-putted a green, by the time they tell me the distance to the hole I am already on the next tee.

BALL ON THE FAIRWAY

It is worth repeating this rule again: Absent a few discrete exceptions, the only time a golf ball is allowed to be picked up during a round is when you're on the green (except, of course, if you are picking up your ball because you already lie ten and you're still half a mile from the green).

Obviously, another exception is if you are in a penalty situation, because you need to pick up the ball in order to drop it. You can also pick it up to determine if it is "unfit for play" (probably not the reason you only hit the ball ten feet), to identify whether or not it's yours, or because it is interfering with someone else's ability to play his or her ball (meaning it is right in the line of the other player's ball). The best policy is to never pick up your ball unless — or until — you are on the green and only if you have absolutely no alternative but to do so. And if you intend to pick up your ball anywhere other than the green, to avoid a challenge as to the "legality" of your action, confer with the other players to confirm their agreement that you are doing the right thing.

Oh, did I say those are the only times you can pick up your ball? Well, there are a few others: When the course is especially wet, or has just been "aerated" (meaning that holes have been punched on the surface to let the air circulate within the ground), the course superintendent will allow all players to "pick, clean, and place" their ball. That basically signifies that you can legally pick up your ball, wipe it off, and place it back down precisely where it was. No more, no less. But you can only do this on the fairway: Not the first cut, not the rough, not in the sand trap. Only on the fairway and only if the course has established this policy for the day.

Another exception to the rule: If your ball is sailing through the air and it comes down so straight and hard that it "plugs" into the wet ground (meaning you can see the top of it sticking out, but it requires an ice cream scoop to pull it out), you are allowed to pull it out of the plug, clean it, and drop it without counting it as a stroke. Okay, enough exceptions to the rule for now.

It is worth reiterating that when you dig that trench in the fairway by that beautiful shot to the green with your 7-iron, you should do what you can to repair the divot left in the ground. If you have a sand/seed mixture on your cart, fill in the divot, smooth it out with your foot, and you can be on your way. If the piece of earth you excavated is lying ten feet away and you don't have a sand/seed mixture, by all means go retrieve the sod and replace it, as well as you can, on the divot. That being said, I have been told by some groundskeepers that replacing the sod in the divot rarely works and, eventually, you will have a section of dead grass in the middle of the fairway. Others insist that if you replace the sod immediately it can and will grow back. My view is that you lose nothing by replacing the divot, and grass — even dead grass — looks a lot better than bare earth. If the next golfer's ball happens to roll where your ball was, it will be easier for him to hit it if you've repaired the divot. Also, it shows that you care about the condition of the course if you take the time to replace the sod. One final caveat: Be aware of those hitting around you. If someone's ball is parallel to yours, let him shoot first before you retrieve the sod. It's better than rushing forward and possibly being exposed to an errant shot.

HITTING ON ANOTHER FAIRWAY

If you are playing on a links-type course, you may find your errant shot is on the adjoining fairway. This is much better than it being in a hazard, lost, or out of bounds because (unlike those three tragedies) you may hit your next shot without penalty! However, that also means that the group on that adjoining hole may be hitting towards you. So what should you do? Run down and hit your ball as fast as you can so your group doesn't glare at you for slowing down their pace of play? Nope. It's like making a left turn with traffic coming from the opposite direction. If you cut in front of an oncoming car, things will not fare well for you. It's the same as hitting from another fairway with the "legitimate" golfers traveling in your direction.

If you are on another fairway, the group that's already there has the right of way. Period. Often that group will recognize the need for you to hit and get out of the way, but if they don't, you are out of luck. You must wait until they have hit their balls and cleared the way for you to go to your ball and hit it (hopefully) back onto your fairway. Once again, this is why it is so important for you to mark your ball so you are able to clearly recognize your Titleist from other balls of the some brand that are on the fairway. Not only can it be embarrassing to hit a ball onto their fairway, but then hitting their ball back onto your fairway is almost as bad as making that left turn into ongoing traffic. Mark your ball so that you can recognize it, let the group on their own fairway have the right away, and hustle to catch up and keep up with your group (which means picking up your ball if you have to. Sorry.).

POWER CARTS

Let's talk a little more about power carts. If you are riding a cart, you have to be aware of the cart rules for the day. Your options include "cart path only," the "90-degree rule," or "anything goes"(within reason, that is).

"Cart path only" is exactly what it says: Your cart must always remain on the cart path. That means always. Not sometimes. Not most of the time. Always. This is usually because the course is wet and driving the cart on the course will cause damage to the grass. As you will note from the acknowledgments in this book, I am lucky enough to count among my favorite golfing partners the former governor of Maine, John Baldacci. Now that he is no longer the governor (and he can't pardon me for some future crime), I can tell you that, on occasion, he declared, by executive order, the "cart path only" rule invalid if his ball and my ball were more than one hundred yards away from each other. Of course, now that he is no longer the governor we have both lost this privilege.

If you are using a cart and it is cart path only on the day you are playing, and your ball is on the other side of the fairway (and, by the way, Murphy's Law says this will happen 90 percent of the time), you should always try to guestimate how far you are from the tee and what club you are going to need for your next shot. Then always — always, always, always — take at least one club longer and one club shorter than the one you think you are going to use. You do not want to walk all the way over to the other side of the fairway just to discover that you really need your

8-iron instead of your 7-iron. You'd then have to walk all the way back to the cart to retrieve the correct club and all the way back to the ball again to hit it. Remember glaring golfers? This is a needless slowing down of the game. Bring a few clubs with you and be safe.

The "90-degree rule" means that the course is somewhat wet but that the superintendent has determined that some cart movement on the course will not substantially damage the grass. The 90-degree rule is accomplished by driving your cart on the cart path until you turn your cart at a 90-degree angle to head directly to your ball. Obviously, at some point you are going to have to turn your cart around and head back to the cart path. But if you keep to the routine of driving on the cart path until you are even with your ball, turning 90 degrees and going to your ball, and then turning around and heading back to the cart path, you'll have mastered the art of driving 90 degrees!

A golfer follows the "90-degree rule" entering the fairway.

Note that if your cart partner's ball is twenty yards ahead of yours, do not go to your ball and then sneak twenty yards forward on the fairway before turning back to the cart path. You know better than that; that's not

90-degree driving! You either go back to the cart path, drive twenty more yards, and then head out to your partner's ball at a 90-degree angle, or you just tell your lazy partner to walk to his damn ball and then walk back to the cart. Then you'll both drive back to the cart path and, hopefully, forward towards the green.

If the course is in good shape and there is no potential damage to the grass, the course will allow you to drive the cart anywhere on the fairway your little heart desires. That being said, use some common sense: Be careful around sand traps and hazards (it would be really embarrassing to drive a power cart into a sand trap and dangerous to drive it over a cliff). And never — never, never, never — get close to the green with your cart. As a general rule, never drive your cart closer than thirty yards from the green. When you get that close to it, head to the cart path and pull up where carts belong, on the side of the green. Most courses will have markers on the fairway, before you reach the green, showing you when you can advance no further toward the flag with your golf cart. When you see these markers, do not go past them under any circumstances.

By the way, I have never seen a course that allows you to go on the fairway on a par-3 hole. So as a general rule, stay on the cart path on a par 3, no matter what the condition of the fairway.

Also, keep in mind that a golf course is not a racetrack. The goal is to get your ball to the green with the fewest number of strokes, not to beat everyone else to the green by power-cart racing. Drive responsibly. It is very easy to get hurt, or to hurt your partner, on a golf cart. A precipitous turn to the left when your rider isn't looking could easily result in the seat next to you suddenly becoming empty. And if you are the rider, all carts have handles that you can grab onto if the driver of your cart is practicing for the Indianapolis 500. If your partner insists on driving recklessly, switch places with him and you drive. You would not get into a car with a reckless driver; no reason to make your round of golf any more treacherous.

POWER-CART POSITION

Is there power-cart etiquette? Of course! Your cart should be positioned generally the same way as you stood on the tee when your golfing partners hit their shots — at a 45-degree angle back but within their eyesight. A cart parallel to the golfer is probably not going to cause him a major distraction, but just keep the cart as inconspicuous as a vehicle standing in the middle of the fairway can be.

Needless to say, when your cart partner is preparing to hit, it is not the time to eat loudly, rattle your clubs, call your broker, or mutter under your breath about the bad luck you experienced when your last shot hit that tree. You should act no differently than you would on the tee: Quietly and deferentially. Then, if your partner makes a bad shot, it's not your fault. Do you get the idea that this is all about avoiding blame?

POWER-CART MOVEMENT

Keeping within the spirit of ready golf, you and your riding partner do not have to go to every ball together, then wait until each hits his or her respective shots, and repeat this for eighteen holes. It is perfectly logical for one player to drop the other player off at his ball and then take the cart to another destination. This is particularly appropriate when one partner has to hunt for his golf ball: Drop the other player where he thinks his ball entered the twilight zone, take the cart to your ball, and then go back and pick up your partner after you have made your shot. Or have him drop you off first and he can take the cart to go look for his ball. It doesn't really matter. What's important is to play ready golf — and to do this you won't be able to go to every ball location together every time.

GARY PLAYER IS KNOWN AS "THE WORLD'S MOST TRAVELED ATHLETE" FOR RACKING UP MORE THAN 14 MILLION MILES GOING TO COURSES AROUND THE GLOBE DURING HIS CAREER.

When you get close to the green, one of your balls may be on the other side of the fairway and too close to the green to drive up to the ball. It's easy to manage the cart: The player on the far side of the fairway gets dropped off as close to his ball as the markers will allow and the other player brings the cart to the cart path and up to the green where the cart is supposed to be parked. Just use your common sense when managing two players and one power cart. Also, if you are dropping your partner off, remember to bring your partner's putter to the green with you if he doesn't already have it with him so he doesn't have to go back to the cart to retrieve his putter. Ready golf! Finally, if it is a hot day, park your cart under a tree (unless, of course, you have to drive to the next hole to find a tree). Parking in the shade will keep your cart (and you) cooler.

PUSHCARTS

Because a pushcart is not a vehicle (and, therefore, less likely to cause damage to a fairway), it does not have to follow the rules for power carts. This saves time since it's much faster to meander down the fairway with your pushcart than to have to park the power cart on the cart path and walk to your ball all the time.

But the rule about power carts around the green applies to pushcarts, too. Although you can bring your pushcart right up to the edge of the green, keep it a reasonable distance from the fringe of the green, and never, never, never push your cart, or set your bag, onto the surface of the green.

LOOKING FOR YOUR BALL

Under the rules of golf, you may look for a lost ball for five minutes. However, we are not professionals, so we are not bound by such mundane rules. We can look for a lost ball for hours, right? Not!

Take my word for it: If you don't readily find your ball in a hazard in the first thirty seconds of your search, you are probably not going to find it at all. You may find someone else's, but that doesn't count as your ball.

That also doesn't mean you shouldn't take a few minutes to look for a lost ball. Just be conscious of the pace of play. If you are far ahead of the group behind you or others are searching for their lost balls, by all means take a few extra minutes to look for yours if you think you can find it.

But if your ball has flown five miles over the highway adjoining the golf course, use some common sense. Take two or three minutes to look for your ball and then call it quits. If your ball is that well-hidden, it's probably not easily playable anyway. Yes, you don't want to lose a ball that cost you $4.00, but if you are losing a lot of balls you probably shouldn't be playing with expensive ones!

LOOKING FOR SOMEONE ELSE'S BALL

It is basic golf courtesy to assist other golfers looking for their wayward balls. Yes, even if you are playing in a match against them. It is amazing how helpful other players will be in finding your ball if you show a little courtesy in helping them hunt for theirs. Also, it will speed up play if more than one set of eyes is looking for a ball. My rule of thumb is to help look for a ball for two or three minutes and, if not found, move on. I follow that same rule when it is my ball I am looking for: Two or three minutes, a thank you for those who helped look for it, and time to move on.

BALL ON THE CART PATH

If your ball ends up on a cart path, congratulations. This is much better than losing it. And guess what? You get to drop the ball off of the cart path! You are not required to hit it off the cart path (although you may if you wish). You are not even required to stand on the cart path to hit a ball that lies just off the path.

Actually, the formal process for taking relief off a cart path is incredibly methodical and I would be doing you a disservice if I didn't outline for you the way it is supposed to be done. Then I will tell you how to really do it, particularly in an informal game.

Follow me here: You are supposed to go to the right side of the cart path, stand completely off the cart path (this will probably be about one yard from the cart path), take the club you intend to play from this distance, take your stance as if you were going to hit a ball (which isn't even on the ground at this point), and put a tee where your clubhead touches the ground. You do the same thing on the left side of the cart path. This will not be a yard from the cart path because, assuming you are a right-handed golfer, the clubhead is closer to the cart path than your tee.

You then determine which tee is closer to your ball (which is still on the cart path). You stand on that tee and drop your ball within one club-length of that point, no closer to the hole, and not in a hazard, or on a green, and at a point at which the cart path no longer interferes with your swing or your stance. By the way, to drop the ball you extend your arm at a 90-degree angle in a manner so that the ball falls and lands no closer to the hole and doesn't roll back on the cart path (hopefully). And, to reiterate, you must take "complete" relief. What does this mean? Simply that you cannot stand on the path and hit the ball that you've dropped off the path, nor can you drop the ball so it remains on the cart path even though your feet are off the path. You and the ball must be completely off the cart path.

Okay, now the easy method. Remember when I said earlier that dropping off the right-side of the cart path will be farther away (for a right-handed golfer) because you have to stand off the cart path first, then take your stance, then put a tee where your clubhead meets the ground? That will put the tee farther away from the cart path than on the left side, where the clubhead will be relatively close to the cart path because your feet are farther away from the path. Right? So unless the cart path is unusually wide and the ball is all the way on the right side of the path, the nearest point of relief will almost always be the left side of the cart path for right-handed golfers (and the right side of the cart path for left-handed golfers). So unless you are playing with the most obsessive-compulsive golfers in the world, just plant the tee on the left side of the cart path and drop the ball within one club-length of where you are standing, as described above.

If your dropped ball rolls closer to the pin or back onto the cart path, you'll need to repeat this exercise all over again. If it rolls closer to the pin or back onto the cart path a second time, no, you don't go for a third strike. You place the ball where it first touched the grass on the second drop. Whew, all that just to get off the cart path!

SAND TRAPS

Yes, I hate sand traps, too. Especially fairway sand traps. But a few words about the care and maintenance of sand traps: Before you go into the sand trap to hit the ball, find the nearest rake and bring it to the side of the sand trap from which you entered. With steep traps you should enter from a low spot. This is because, as you would quickly find out, if you enter from a deep spot you will slide down the sand and have more sand in your shoes than in the trap.

You are not allowed to "ground" your club in the sand trap. This means your club is not allowed to touch the ground in the sand trap until you are actually swinging at the ball.

You can't ground your club in a hazard or sand trap.

After you hit the ball out of the sand trap (no comment about how many times it may take you to do that), take the rake and make the sand trap as smooth as you can. Rake where your feet dug into the sand, and where your club struck the sand. On the way out of the trap, rake your footprints, too. Don't rush raking the sand. Not only is it courteous to leave the trap as pristine as you should have found it, it is also a good time to relax, to take a deep breath, and to get in touch with your inner self. It's just like a Zen garden. It may help you forget the three strokes it took you to get out of the trap. It's like chanting to the universe. Ohmmmmmmmmmmm. Okay, back to planet earth. Don't go crazy, but smooth it out as much as possible and leave as little evidence as you can that you were even there. You want to be conscious of ready play, but at the same time you don't want the next golfer who hits in the sand to be cursing the dolt who left a giant footprint there, where his ball now lies.

A rake pointing to the tee box minimizes the chances of it stopping your ball.

There are actually two "philosophies" about where to put the rake. Some clubs want the rake left in the sand trap, some outside the sand trap. The best way to avoid going wrong is to leave it wherever you found it. I think there is more logic to leaving the rake in the trap: A rake outside of the trap can stop a ball from going into the trap. Nice for you, but not really the way the game is supposed to be played. A rake in the trap may stop the ball from going further into the trap, but will not likely keep the ball out of the sand.

Finally, no matter if the rake is in or out of the trap, I always lay it down so that the handle is pointing to the tee box. Why? So if someone hits his or her ball toward the sand trap, you have made the rake the smallest target that can possibly stop or divert that ball. Of course, make sure the rake prongs are pointed down to the ground. And don't stand by the sand trap cleaning the sand off your club. You have plenty of time to clean it as you walk to your cart or prepare for your next shot.

HITTING SOMEONE ELSE'S BALL

Always, always, always look at your ball before you hit it. No, you are not allowed to pick up your ball to examine it, clean it, and put it down in a better lie. But you should be able to look at it as it lies there waiting to be hit and determine if it is your ball or not (particularly if you marked your ball as I begged you to do two chapters ago. See how all of this comes full circle?). Not only is there a severe penalty for hitting the wrong ball (two strokes), but it is simply an unnecessary mistake. Know what ball you are hitting and check it before you hit it and life will be grand.

WHEN YOUR BALL HITS ANOTHER BALL

This is different from you hitting someone else's ball that you think is yours. This is when you hit your own ball, but it accidentally hits another person's ball. Although this is rare any place on the golf course other than the green (discussed later), it is easy to correct. You play your ball from where it ends up after it collided with the other ball. The owner of that ball returns it to his best estimate of where it was when yours hit it. No penalty. No harm, no foul.

WHEN A BALL MOVES

Ah, but not so easy if your ball moves before you hit it. Remember that on the tee box, if your ball moves for any reason other than that you actually tried to hit it, it doesn't count as a stroke. Not so on the fairway (or the green). If you, a playing partner, a caddy, or your equipment accidentally causes your ball to move, that is trouble with a capital "T." One-stroke penalty. Yes, really. Even if you didn't do it. Even if it was an accident. And this applies if you move a pine cone next to your ball and it causes a twig to spring forth and move your ball just a tiny bit. Tough luck. Intention has nothing to do with it. One-stroke penalty. Suck it up and move on.

HAZARDS

There are three basic hazards you may encounter on a hole of golf. All hazards are designated by a line of stakes that separate the playable golf course surfaces from the "I hit a really bad shot" side of the golf course. The three basic hazards are: 1) out of bounds (white-staked hazards), 2) lateral hazards (red-staked hazards), and 3) water hazards (yellow-staked hazards). It's important to keep in mind that a lateral hazard can be caused by water and a yellow hazard doesn't have to have water to be a yellow hazard even though it's called a water hazard. Don't ask why, just go with the flow here.

If you lose your ball and it does not go into one of the three hazard areas described above, it is a lost ball. A lost ball is treated in the same way as a ball that goes out of bounds.

OUT OF BOUNDS

Out of bounds is indicated by a line of white stakes. It is very common for out of bounds to be protection for a homeowner next to a golf course. In other words, if a house is on a fairway, there will likely be a line of white stakes following the property line. Two white stakes stuck in the ground together will denote the beginning of the out of bounds section and two white stakes will denote the end of an out of bounds section. Then, between the beginning and end of the out of bounds section there will be a series of single white stakes separating in bounds from hell.

Out of bounds is out of luck.

Remember how you drew an imaginary line between the two markers on the tee box so that you would not tee your ball in front of the marker? Well, you do the same thing in all hazards: You draw an imaginary line between the two stakes and if your ball is completely on the other side of that imaginary line, it's in the hazard. This is worth repeating: The entire ball must be on the other side of that imaginary line for it to be in the hazard. This is a judgment call, but since, once again, golf is the only game in which the player calls a penalty on himself, you are trusted to make the right call. It may not matter if the ball is three inches into a red or yellow hazard, because, as you will learn in a minute, you are allowed to attempt to hit out of a red- or yellow-staked hazard. But it makes a huge difference if your ball is out of bounds, because you are never allowed to hit your ball back in bounds, even if you find it, see it, and can hit it safely. If your ball is out of bounds, you are not allowed to hit it back in bounds. Ever. Period. Exclamation point. You don't have to leave your ball in the out of bounds area, but you can't hit it back into play.

So if your ball goes out of bounds and you can't hit it back in bounds from where it ended up, where do you hit it from? From the original spot from whence you hit your wayward ball. And that is why, if you are pretty sure you hit your ball out of bounds (or that it's lost), you take a second shot, known as a "provisional," before you head out looking for your first ball.

You have to declare your second ball as a provisional ("I am hitting a provisional ball!") and you have to make sure you can identify it from the original ball (because if you hit a provisional ball and then find your original ball, you can resume play with your original ball, without penalty, if it is legally playable). You can (and should) hit a provisional ball any time you think it is prudent to do so to avoid having to walk all the way back to your original spot.

If you hit a ball out of bounds, or you lose your ball, the penalty is "stroke and distance." This means you count one stroke for hitting the ball out of bounds or losing your ball, one stroke for returning to the scene of the crime (where you were when you hit the ball badly), and a third shot to put your ball back in play. That means, assuming your second hit doesn't go out of bounds again, you will be "lying three" and your next hit will be your fourth shot (and if you end up playing your provisional ball you would, of course, lie three). Sounds draconian and unfair, I admit, but those are the rules. As you will quickly learn, the rules of golf are not always fair or rational. By the way, before you hit a second ball from the tee, either as a provisional or because you know your ball went out of bounds or was lost, you may tee it up again. However, remember that the *only* time you can tee up your ball is when you hit it from the tee box, either on your drive or when you take a second drive due to a lost ball. So if your first drive was playable and it was your second shot that went out of bounds, you cannot tee up your correcting shot from the fairway, just as you can never tee up any shot from the fairway.

Once again, a lost ball is treated in the same way as a ball out of bounds. The only real difference between a lost ball and a ball out of bounds is that if you can find your ball that went out of bounds you haven't lost the cost of a golf ball because you can play it in the future. And before we launch into red- and yellow-staked hazards, the good news is that if you lose your ball in one of those hazards, you only incur a one-stroke penalty instead of the "stroke and distance" penalty that results from a ball that goes out of bounds or is lost.

RED-STAKED HAZARDS

A red-staked hazard is defined as a lateral water hazard, which means it stakes out those areas on either side of the fairway where you are likely to find water (or where water used to be). In a moment you will read about yellow-staked areas, which denotes a water hazard in front of you instead of parallel to the fairway. One of the ironies of red-staked and yellow-staked areas is that despite the fact of being called a water hazard, the nearest water could be a fountain on the next tee. Just one of the mysteries of golf.

But a red stake is much better than a white stake because, as stated above, the major difference between the two is that a ball in a red-staked hazard can be played out of the hazard, but a ball out of bounds may never be played even if you find it and it is perfectly playable. This doesn't mean you have to or you should hit a ball from a red-staked hazard; it just means you can if you want to. Even if you have a clear shot to the green from the hazard, you do not have to hit it out of the hazard if you don't want to. If you do decide to hit your ball, you are not allowed to ground your club in the hazard. You must hover your club above the ball until your striking swing.

If you decide not to hit a ball from the hazard, your penalty is one stroke. And contrary to what you do if you lose a ball or hit a ball out of bounds, you do not return to where you hit the original errant shot to make your next shot: You drop your ball where you believe the ball crossed the hazard line, no closer to the hole.

Okay, so follow me on this: First, when you hit your ball and you realize it may be heading into a hazard, you have to do the best you can to estimate where the ball is entering the hazard area. It is easier to determine this point of entry if and when you ultimately find your ball. You can just look back from where you first hit the ball to where it landed to figure out where it crossed the line. But if you can't find your ball, you have to do the best you can to estimate the point at which your ball first crossed into the hazard.

Often the line between two red stakes will actually be marked by a red line on the ground (similar to the white powdered lines on a football field) so that you know where the hazard begins and when a ball is legally in the hazard. The reason why you need a line between the two stakes is to determine the point where you'll be dropping the ball for your next shot. But, first, what if the line from the two hazard stakes is not drawn on the ground (or is too faded to ascertain)? Just as we did with the tee-box markers and the out of bound white stakes, we visualize an imaginary line between the two red stakes in order to determine the likely location where our ball entered the hazard.

Once the line is determined (whether marked by the course or eyeballed by you), if you did not find your ball in the hazard or you found it and decided to not play it from the hazard, you will drop it in almost the same way you did when it was on the cart path. In this case, you drop the ball within two club-lengths from where it crossed into the hazard (that does not mean you stand two club-lengths from the red line and then drop the ball further from the red line — it means the ball has to be dropped within two club-lengths of where your ball crossed the red line into the hazard and no closer to the pin. Then you drop your ball the same as you do on the cart path: You extend your arm at a 90-degree angle and drop the ball no closer to the hole than the point of entry into the red-staked area and within two club-lengths of that entry point.

And what if the ball rolls back into the hazard? I can hear you say, "Don't tell me this is another penalty. I haven't even taken another shot yet!" Nope, stop whining. You're in luck. No second penalty. If the ball rolls back into the hazard after you've dropped it in the legal manner described above (or if it rolls closer to the pin), you simply pick it up again and drop it again. If it rolls closer to the hole or back into the hazard on the second drop, you now place it on the ground as close as possible to where the ball hit the ground on your second drop. Simple, huh?

YELLOW-STAKED HAZARDS

As mentioned above, yellow-staked hazards denote a water hazard that is in front of you rather than to the side of you. Although the yellow stakes may be bordering water, they could be denoting a dried up riverbed, a sea of cacti, or a pit of alligators. The point is that the hazard is in front of you instead of beside you and it is marked with yellow stakes.

The yellow-staked hazard meets the red-staked hazard. Not good in either situation.

You can have red- and yellow-staked hazards in close proximity to each other. For example, if the lateral hazard is a pond on the left side of the fairway, but that pond has "fingers" jutting into the fairway, the fingers would likely be yellow-staked while the part of the pond parallel to the fairway would be red-staked. You can also have a red-staked hazard and an out-of-bounds staked-area right next to each other, too. One can begin where the other ends. Make sure you know which hazard you have gone into because, as you now know, the penalty for each is very different.

The out of bounds ends and the red-staked hazard begins.

Almost every aspect of the yellow-staked hazard is identical to the red-staked hazard. When you hit your ball and you think it may be heading into the hazard, you need to estimate where it entered the hazard. You can hit out of a yellow hazard if you are able to, but the choice is entirely yours. Yellow-staked areas can have a yellow line on the ground dividing the playing ground from the hazard area.

The major difference between a red-staked and a yellow-staked hazard is that when you are dropping a ball from a yellow-staked hazard, you can actually move and drop your ball as far back as you want to, so long as the ball is not dropped any closer to the hole (instead of being restricted to two club-lengths from the line between the two yellow stakes). From a yellow-staked hazard you can drop your ball fifty yards back toward the tee box if for some masochistic reason you choose to do so. The more logical reason is that if you find the grass is rough close to the entrance of the yellow-staked hazard, and that by going back another five yards you'd be hitting from the fairway, you are then free to opt for the fairway rather than the rough. See, you may not be so masochistic after all!

One other point about red- and yellow-staked hazards: If you choose to try to hit your ball from either hazard and you fail to do so, you don't get a do-over. It counts as a stroke and you are no better off than you were before you tried to hit it out in the first place. So sometimes it's better to just take your medicine like a golfer, drop your ball out of the hazard, and suck up the one-stroke penalty. Tell yourself that it could have been worse: You could have hit your ball out of bounds!

UNPLAYABLE LIES

If your ball lands in a place where no one would have ever thought a ball could land (or be hit from), but 1) it is not lost (lucky you, you found it); 2) it is not out of bounds (lucky you, you saved a two-stroke penalty); and 3) it is not in a red-or yellow-staked hazard, you may still declare it "unplayable." This means you can see it, but you really can't, or don't want to, play it. It is on a rock, in the crook of a tree, or under a spiny bush. You get the point. It is a ball that you cannot strike with your club without either hurting your club or yourself.

You have three alternatives if your ball is unplayable, which actually combine the option you're given if your ball is hit out of bounds with the option you're given if you hit your ball into a red- or yellow-staked hazard: 1) You can return the ball to where it was when you first hit it; 2) you can drop the ball within two club-lengths of where the ball came to rest, but no closer to the pin; or 3) you can drop the ball behind the point where the ball came to rest, as far back as you wish to go. All three alternatives result in a one-stroke penalty. Now that I have told you the logical definition of an unplayable lie, let me

An unplayable lie can be hazardous to your health. And to your club.

admit that I actually lied about what an unplayable lie is. It doesn't *have* to be unplayable. It can be playable by you or anyone else. You can declare a ball unplayable even if it is perfectly playable, if you don't mind getting a one-stroke penalty. Now why would anyone want to call a ball unplayable if it is perfectly playable? Other than to just show off that you know this rule, there really is no logical reason to make such a call. I suppose if you are playing a match-play tournament, and you already have seven strokes on the hole and you assume you'll never recover to win it, and your ball is buried three inches in the sand trap, and you don't have the energy to try to hit it out, you may declare it unplayable just to make your life easier. Which brings up a final point about unplayable lies: You cannot move the ball two club-lengths out of a sand trap. You can exercise all of the other options for relief from an unplayable lie, within the sand trap, but if you want to move your ball out of the sand trap you must return the ball to where it was when you first hit it.

So here are the revised rules of the unplayable lie:

- You have the sole authority to declare a ball unplayable.
- You can declare a ball unplayable anywhere on the course other than in a water or lateral hazard.

Take advantage of "ground under repair" and drop your ball for a better lie.

- You can only move your ball out of a sand trap by declaring it unplayable if you move it to where you first hit it.
- When you call a ball unplayable you are penalized one stroke. You get two things for that penalty: You get to clean your ball and you get a playable lie. A bargain if ever there was one.

GROUND UNDER REPAIR

Often, the groundskeeper will identify areas of the golf course that need to be repaired and, therefore, they don't want you whacking away at your ball and making a particular section worse. They will circle the area they wish to protect with a white line. Not a problem. You simply pick up your ball, identify the nearest point of relief (remember the cart path rule?), and drop it within one club-length of that point. This is, of course, another exception to the "never, never, never pick up your ball on the course unless it's on the green" rule. But, as we know, every rule has its exceptions. And another irony about the "ground under repair" rule is that unless the course specifies that you *have* to drop your ball outside of the area marked as a ground under repair, you may hit it from within the marked area if you want to. I don't know why you would want to, but maybe you think it looks like a better place to hit from than your closest point of relief. In any event, it is your call.

OTHER COLORED STAKES

Believe it or not, there are blue stakes and green stakes too. But I have only seen a green stake once and I have never seen a blue stake. However, just so you know something that probably no one else on your team will know, a blue stake is another way to denote "ground under repair" and a green stake demarcates an "environmentally sensitive area."

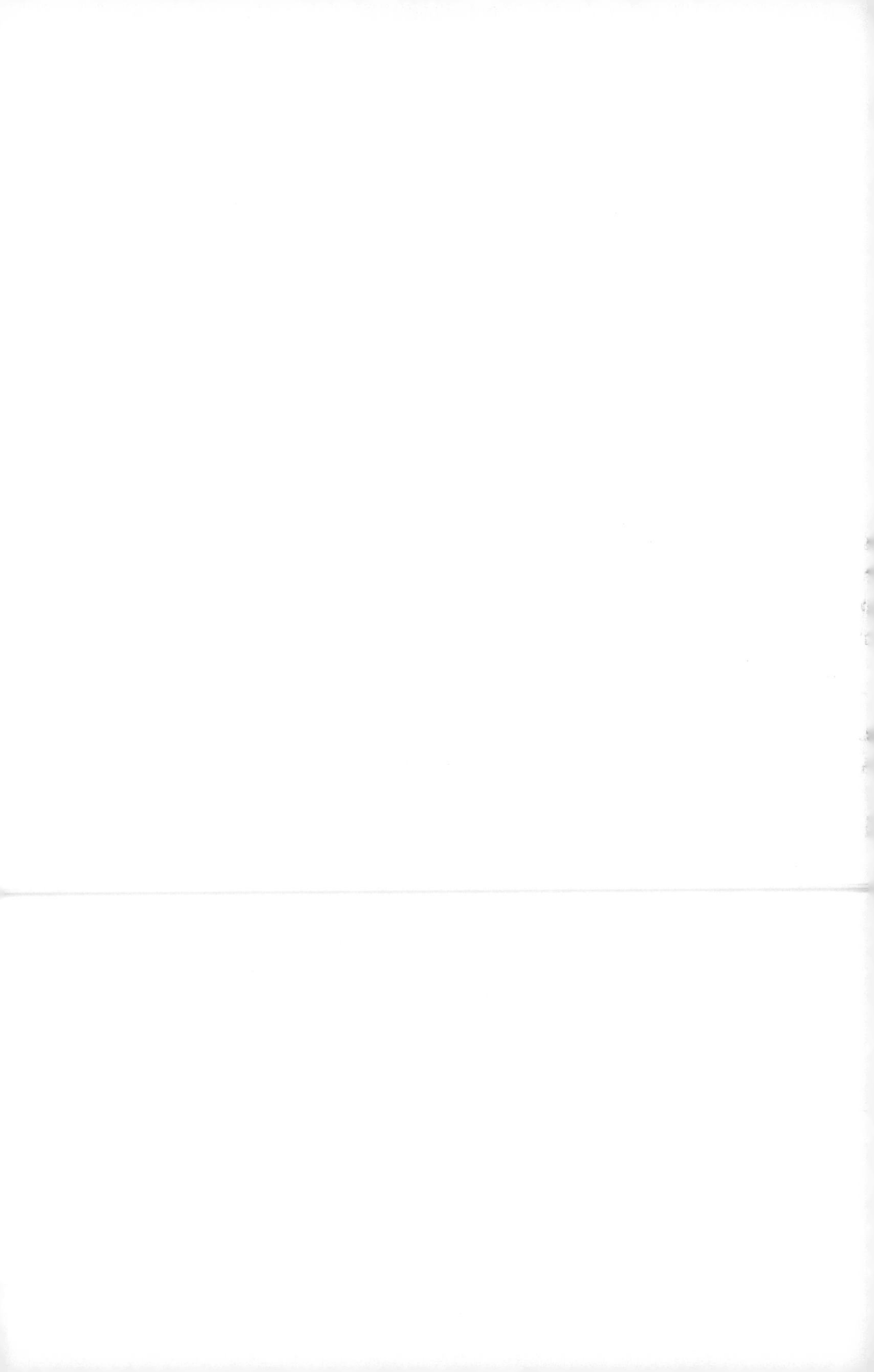

A JOKE TO TELL WHILE YOU'RE SCORING THE MATCH.

JAMES AND CHARLIE WERE PLAYING GOLF AT THEIR FAVORITE COURSE. HOWEVER, ON EVERY HOLE THEY WERE HELD UP BY A VERY SLOW TWOSOME OF WOMEN WHO WERE ALWAYS A HALF HOLE AHEAD OF THEM.

FINALLY, AFTER WATCHING THE WOMEN IN THE DISTANCE AS THEY LINED UP THEIR PUTTS FOR WHAT SEEMED TO BE AN ETERNITY, CHARLIE DECIDED THAT ACTION MUST BE TAKEN.

"I'M GOING TO WALK UP THERE AND ASK THEM IF WE CAN PLAY THROUGH." CHARLIE SAID, HEADING OFF DOWN THE FAIRWAY, TOWARDS THE WOMEN. BUT WHEN HE GOT HALFWAY THERE, HE STOPPED, TURNED AROUND, AND HEADED BACK TO WHERE JAMES WAS WAITING.

"I CAN'T GO UP THERE," CHARLIE SAID, SHEEPISHLY. "ONE OF THEM IS MY WIFE AND THE OTHER IS MY MISTRESS!"

"OKAY," JAMES SAID UNDERSTANDINGLY. "I'LL GO UP AND ASK THEM."

JAMES STARTED UP THE FAIRWAY, ONLY TO STOP HALFWAY AND TURN AROUND.

WHAT'S WRONG?" CHARLIE ASKED WHEN JAMES RETURNED.

JAMES REPLIED, "SMALL WORLD, ISN'T IT?"

Chapter 14

Golf's Holy Grail: On the Green

PREPARING FOR THE NEXT HOLE

If you are walking, either carrying a bag or with a pushcart, think about where the next tee box is and endeavor to place your bag somewhere between the flag on your current green and the next tee box. Once again, never, never, never (that means never) place your golf bag or pushcart on the surface of the green. I assume I don't have to tell you again to not drive a power cart onto the green either. Just remember that this area is the most fragile, and most important, playing surface on the entire course. Treat it with reverence.

When you are parking your cart next to the green, park towards the end of the green rather than the beginning. The whole point of where you place your bag or where you park your cart is to maintain the pace of play. You want to be ready to leave the green as soon as everyone has putted out and get to the next tee in a reasonable amount of time and not unnecessarily delay the group behind you. They're supposed to wait until you clear the green completely before hitting so you don't want to put a damper on their fun by taking additional time to clear out.

If you see the group in front of you is teeing off as you approach the next tee, do NOT drive up right behind their carts. Stop your cart (or stop walking if you are not in a cart) a respectful distance away from the tee so that they're not unduly pressured or distracted by your presence. That is particularly helpful if you are in a "friendly discussion" as to whether or not your playing partner counted that duff from 150 yards out. The group in front of you doesn't want or need to participate in that debate.

CUTS OF GRASS

Just as there are different cuts of grass on the fairway, so go the greens. And the same terms apply: The bulk of the green is that smooth, felt-like carpet of greenery that is cut so close to the ground that your ball glides over it as if it is glass.

Around the green is the fringe. The fringe is NOT the green. This is an important distinction, because you are allowed to mark your ball on the green but you are not allowed to mark your ball if it's on the fringe. The only exception to this is if another player is on the fringe as well and your ball is in his line as he hits toward the pin. In this event, you may mark your ball just as you can and would on the green.

Around the fringe is the rough, which is similar, if not identical, to the rough off the fairway. It's just more frustrating to encounter it here because you are so close to the pin and if you'd only hit the ball that extra foot or two, you would have avoided the rough. But that's why they call it rough.

MARKING YOUR BALL

Okay, this is different from marking your ball to be able to identify it on the fairway. This is marking your ball so that you can pick it up from the green and do whatever you want to do to it before you actually putt (such as wiping the mud off of it). You also mark your ball because a white ball on a bright-green green, within eyesight of the player putting, can be distracting. If you want to be courteous to others, mark your ball on the green until it is your time to putt.

Along with a tool to repair ball marks, you should always have in your pocket something to mark where your ball is on the green. But, really, anything that is flat and can be seen by the naked eye can be used as a marker — a quarter, a tiddledywink, or a marker from the Masters. Some golf gloves have a little marker on the wrist snap that can be used in a pinch or as a routine marker if so desired. As is true with the ball mark repair tool, a marker from your favorite golf course will bring back memories of that forty-foot putt you sank on that trip to Hawaii.

Place your marker behind your ball until it is your turn to putt.

Your marker should be placed directly behind where your ball lies on the green (and, by the way, you cannot mark your ball if it is still moving. If you hit on the slope and it starts sliding off the top tier, you can't run and try to mark your ball before it stops). Once you mark your ball you should not place it back on the putting surface until you are ready to putt. Although, as you know, I am a big fan of ready golf, the time to put your ball back on the green is not when someone else is putting. You'll get your turn. By the way, if you legally mark your ball (which means you marked it only after it stopped moving) and then it starts moving again (they call the wind Mariah), you can replace the ball in its original spot without penalty.

MOVING YOUR BALL

If your ball is on or near the putting path of another golfer, it is always courteous for you to offer to move your ball or marker. You never pick up and/or move your ball. You always mark your ball first and then move your marker, not your ball. Now it becomes a tad more complicated. Do not just pick up your marker and move it to the right or left. That's wrong, wrong, wrong. Keep your marker where it is. Ask the other golfer

When moving your ball out of another player's putting path, move your marker, not the ball.

if he wants you to move the marker to the left or right. You use the putter head to move your marker from the other player's putting path. You place one end of the putter head right next to your ball marker (perpendicular to the putting line) and move the marker to the other end of the putter (presumably in the direction in which your opponent wanted the ball moved). After the golfer putts (and assuming the ball actually gets closer to the pin than yours is), replace your marker in the exact opposite manner that you moved your marker as described above. And that's it. Simple, huh?

MARKING SOMEONE ELSE'S BALL

There may be an occasion that you will want to, or be required to, mark another player's golf ball (he hits on the green from a fairly long distance off the green, another foursome is breathing down your backs, and the remaining players want to start putting while the fourth player gets to the green). You can mark the ball for another player. However, the correct procedure after doing this is that when the player is ready to put his ball down again, you are required to replace his ball for him. In other words, if you mark the ball, you replace the ball. But it is always good sportsmanship to ask the other player if you can mark his ball *before* doing so.

REPAIRING BALL MARKS

There is nothing more unsightly than a green with pockmarks all over it (think of your date at the senior prom). It is everyone's responsibility to repair ball marks on the green and your playing partners will be incredibly impressed if they observe you readily repairing your mark (and their mark) or any other mark you see.

Repairing a mark is easy. First, you should be carrying a ball mark repair tool in your pocket during your round. If you don't have one, you can use a tee to repair ball marks, although tools are specifically designed for this purpose. Virtually all pro shops will have ball mark repair tools for free or for a nominal charge. Buy one, carry it with you, and use it frequently.

Insert the repair tool into the outer edge of the mark, with the prongs at a 45-degree angle. Work the turf up and back into place by pushing the tool up and forward. Do this a few times around the sides of the dent until there is enough material to fill the hole. Then stand up, take your putter, pat down the repaired area until it is as smooth as its surroundings, and it will heal quickly. A mark that's treated immediately will heal within days. Every day that goes by without the mark being repaired will exponentially delay the healing process. Make this a chronic habit of yours. It will make the course nicer.

HITTING ANOTHER BALL ON THE GREEN

I already told you that in the rare case your ball hits another ball on the fairway, you simply play your ball where it ends up, and the other player returns her ball to where it was before you so rudely hit it. The same applies if you hit your ball from off the green and it strikes another ball on the green, which, obviously, has not been marked by another player because, presumably, your partner hasn't reached the green yet to mark her ball. No problem. The same rule applies: You play your ball from where it ends up and the person whose ball you hit returns it to her best estimate of where it was on the green before you took your shot.

But notice I said "if you hit your ball from off the green and it strikes another ball on the green." If your ball is already on the green, and when you putt it, it hits another player's ball on the green, then you receive a two-stroke penalty for having the audacity to hit the other ball. Now that is rude. And to make matters worse, there is no penalty to the other player for allowing his ball to be hit by you! A player does not have to voluntarily mark his ball if he doesn't want to, even if he should.

However, you can require him to mark his ball before you putt precisely so you can avoid incurring a penalty for his for his oppositional behavior. By the way, in a match a team may actually utilize a strategy of one player purposely not marking her ball so it can be used as a "backstop" to prevent the other teammate's ball from flying by if hit too hard. However, it is against the rules to do this on purpose. Which means if you say to your partner, "Don't mark your ball so if I hit my ball too hard your ball may stop it," you are in violation of the rules of golf (and disqualified from the hole in match play). If your partner simply "forgets" to mark her ball and your ball "happens" to hit it, you cannot be accused of conspiring to use her ball as a backstop. Wink, wink. Who says golfers are incapable of being sneaky?

BALL, DEFLECTED

And while we're at it, what happens if your ball is stopped or deflected while in motion? Of course, as is true with all golf questions, the answer is: "It depends." If your ball is stopped or deflected by you, your partner, your caddie, or by any other means (for example, a club left on the ground or a stretched foot), you play the ball where it lies after it stops but you are penalized one stroke. If someone else (such as an opponent) causes your ball to be stopped or deflected, you play your ball wherever it ends up but you are not penalized. (If you are playing a match-play tournament and your opponent or his caddie deflects the ball, you have the option to play the ball again from its original spot. If it's a stroke-play tournament and your ball is deflected, you must replay it).

WALKING ON ANOTHER'S PUTTING LINE

Nothing will garner a dirty stare from a playing partner faster than if you step on the line his putt is likely to follow (even if he is forty feet away and there's not a chance in hell he's going to sink the putt). Be conscious of where other balls lie when you are strolling around the green and avoid walking on the line between those balls and the hole. If practical, walk around the other balls to get to where you're going. If that is not practical, the closer you are to the flag when you move from one side to the other, the more likely it will be that you'll avoid stepping on someone else's putting line. In addition to not stepping on his actual putting line, be sure that you're also not crossing in front of his putting line of sight. Walking around and behind him in this situation would be basic courtesy.

ORDER OF PUTTING

As mentioned in chapter twelve, the guiding principle of the order of play is that the person who is farthest from the pin plays first. That rule can become more interesting around the green.

If your ball is off the green (which includes the fringe of the green), you have the option of having the pin remain in the hole, or having the flag tended (as described on page 160), or pulled out completely. Although it is completely up to your discretion, most experts believe that there is a slight advantage to leaving the pin in the hole when you are off the green, particularly if your putt is downhill (the logic being that if you hit the ball too hard and it hits the flag, it will either drop into the hole or bounce very close by).

It is possible (and often happens) that a golfer off the green is closer to the pin than a player on the green. Because the rule is that the person farthest away from the pin putts first, the player off the green is supposed to wait until the person on the green, but farthest from the hole, putts. But that can require that the flag be removed, put back in, then removed again, etc. So let's use some common sense here. My basic rule is that no one putts until everyone is on the green. It really does keep the play moving faster and more smoothly. But don't assume everyone will agree to this. It doesn't hurt to suggest to the golfer farthest away from the flag (but on the green) that you "come onto the green" before he putts. If he says no, let him putt first. And then give him the chapter on ready play. Some golfers take themselves a tad too seriously.

WHERE TO STAND

If you think it's crucial to know where to stand while a player is on the tee box, just imagine how important it is to know where to plant your feet on the green when a player is putting. First and foremost, don't move. Don't move a muscle. Don't breathe — at least not while someone is putting. The point is not to do anything to distract the putter, and nothing distracts the putter more than someone else walking around while he is putting.

Draw an imaginary line from the putter to the pin. Extend that line past the pin and behind the putter. Do not stand anywhere on or in close proximity to that putting line. If you are standing opposite the putter (meaning on the line that stretches from the putter, to the flag, and then to you), you will distract the putter. If you stand on that line directly behind the putter she will see you out of the back corner of her eye. Anywhere else is relatively okay, but the more out of sight you are, the more likely it is that you won't be blamed for a teammate missing that three-foot putt. And don't forget to make sure that your shadow does not extend between your partner's ball and the hole. Avoid distracting him in any way possible.

PULLING THE FLAG

If a player chooses to keep the flag in the hole when approaching from off the green, do not pull out the flag. Ever. For any reason. Even if the player shouts at you to pull out the flag. Ignore him. Once the choice is made to keep the flag in the hole, that selection is irreversible.

However, if a player chooses to have the flag tended, the flag must be removed as the ball approaches the hole.

TENDING THE FLAG

The proper way to tend the flag is to grab it, hold it against the pole (to stop it from flapping in the breeze), and to stand to the side of the flag, keeping yourself at arm's length from it (see how many times we hold our arm out at a 90-degree angle!). If the sun is casting the flagstick's shadow onto the green, it is good practice to stand on the side of the flag with the shadow. It reduces the visual distraction around the hole (golfers get distracted easily). If the hole is on an obvious slant from where the putter's ball is, it is best to stand on the low side of the hole while tending the flag. This is logical because the ball is supposed to be approaching the hole from the high side and you can avoid having to step out of the way of the putt if the putter is playing a tad too aggressively. Once again, if the player asks for the flag to be tended you must pull the flag as the ball approaches the hole. If the ball hits the flagpole when the player is putting from on the green (versus from on the fringe or off the green) it is a penalty against the putter, not you. That will not make you popular with your golfing partners (although you won't be asked to tend the flag again, if that is your ultimate goal). When you are going to tend the flag it is a good idea to make sure the flagpole slides out easily and won't stick in the hole when you really need it to come out.

Hold the flag and stand on the side of the shadow when "tending" the pin.

After you have ascertained that none of your teammates need the flag tended because the hole is within easy sight of their ball (just ask, "Anyone need the flag tended?"), then just remove the flag completely and place it on the ground. Do not slam the flag to the ground because that can leave marks on the green. Also, do not place the flag behind the hole where it can stop a ball that is putted too hard. Just place the flag gently on the green, somewhere nearby, where it cannot interfere with any putt, until everyone has holed out.

PUTTING OUT

Once again, the standard rule is that the person farthest from the pin putts first. However, to adhere to the philosophy of ready play, it sometimes makes sense for one player to "putt out" before the person farthest from the hole putts. Understand that it is the right of the player farthest from the hole to putt first. Also, keep in mind that if you attempt to putt out after missing your first putt, you may be inclined to putt too quickly on the second, presumably more easy putt (and then you'll get to mutter to yourself that you should have just marked your ball and taken your time). However, to speed play up, you can and should ask the player next in line to play if it is okay for you to putt out. If she agrees, go for it. If she declines, mark your ball and wait for your turn. It's also worth noting that if you are playing a match, an opponent may not want you to putt out until he tries to make his putt, theoretically putting more pressure on you. That's all part of golf gamesmanship.

GIMMIES

If you are playing an informal round of golf, it is likely that if you miss your first putt by an inch or two some other player will "give you the putt." This is called a "gimmie." It's also called courteous golf. If someone gives you the putt and you decide to putt anyway and you miss your putt, you don't get to say, "Well, you gave it to me anyway." Nope. If you miss the putt after it was given to you, you lose the benefit of the gimmie and you added another stroke to your score (and then you get to mutter to yourself that you should have taken the gimmie). So if someone gives you the putt, and you decide to accept the gimmie, pick up the ball and move out of the way for the next putter. I want to note that sometimes there is actually good reason to not accept a gimmie. If you are constantly finding yourself not making six-inch putts, you may want the practice of making a short putt on greens under pressure rather than on practice greens with nothing on the line.

You can give or receive a gimmie from any distance. However, the customary distance from which a gimmie is given is if the ball is "in the leather" of your putter. This means that if you put your putter head in the hole and extend the putter shaft toward your ball, the ball would be in the range that falls somewhere before the putter grip begins. Of course, putter grips are no longer made out of leather, but why get nitpicky? And you don't actually have to put the putter into the hole and do this exercise to see if someone should give you the putt. It is a gift from another player. Don't overanalyze it! Take the putt and thank your generous golf companion. And if you are feeling generous, and you think it is a putt that even you could make, give the other player a gimmie. It speeds up play and makes you more popular as well. Of course, if you are playing a match, be careful as to when to concede a putt — you should probably consult with your playing partner before doing so. On the other hand, you may find that the other team gives you a putt later on because of your generosity now.

To be fair, gimmies are the exception to the rule and golf is designed to require every golfer to hit every shot until it falls into the hole. In a tournament, you shouldn't expect a putt to be given to you (and it is illegal in golf for a putt to be conceded in a stroke-play tournament). Gimmies are solely for informal golf and should only be granted when it's obvious that even a two-year-old could sink the putt.

SCORING

When the hole is finished, someone (or everyone) should write down the individual scores. When I am playing in a match or tournament I ask everyone to tell me their score. If I'm playing in an informal round I offer to keep score for everyone (just because I am a control freak) but if that offer is refused, I mind my own business. It's the best way of keeping out of trouble.

So now you have teed off, played through the fairway, the roughs, the hazards, and reached the green. You have also putted out and recorded your scores. You have repeated this exercise eighteen times. Ah, how could life possibly get better than this!

A JOKE TO TELL WHILE YOU'RE TALLYING YOUR STROKES.

JOYCE TEED OFF FOR HER WEEKLY ROUND OF GOLF AND STARTED WITH AN EAGLE ON THE FIRST HOLE AND A BIRDIE ON THE SECOND. ON THE THIRD HOLE SHE SCORED HER FIRST HOLE-IN-ONE. SHE WAS IN THE ZONE WHEN, ALL OF A SUDDEN, HER CELL PHONE RANG. IT WAS HER FAMILY DOCTOR TELLING HER THAT HER HUSBAND HAD JUST BEEN IN A CAR ACCIDENT AND WAS IN CRITICAL CONDITION. JOYCE TOLD THE DOCTOR TO TELL HER HUSBAND THAT SHE WOULD BE THERE AS SOON AS POSSIBLE.

AS SOON AS SHE HUNG UP SHE REALIZED THAT SHE WAS WELL ON HER WAY TO THE ROUND OF HER LIFE. THE NEXT TWO HOLES WERE ON THE WAY BACK TO THE CLUBHOUSE SO SHE DECIDED SHE WOULDN'T LOSE A LOT OF TIME PLAYING THEM ON HER WAY IN. BUT HER INCREDIBLE PLAY CONTINUED UNABATED AND BEFORE SHE KNEW IT SHE HAD PLAYED ALL EIGHTEEN HOLES.

GUILTILY, SHE RUSHED TO THE HOSPITAL AND SAW THE DOCTOR IN THE HALLWAY. THE DOCTOR WAS OUTRAGED. "YOU CONTINUED TO PLAY GOLF WHILE YOUR HUSBAND WAS LANGUISHING IN THE EMERGENCY ROOM, DIDN'T YOU? WELL, IT IS PROBABLY FITTING THAT YOU DID SO BECAUSE IT MAY BE THE LAST ROUND YOU EVER PLAY. FOR THE REST OF HIS LIFE YOU WILL BE REQUIRED TO GIVE HIM ROUND-THE-CLOCK CARE. HIS IVS WILL HAVE TO BE CHANGED HOURLY AND YOU WILL HAVE TO SPOONFEED HIM THREE TIMES A DAY. SO I HOPE YOU ENJOYED IT WHILE YOU COULD!"

JOYCE FELT SO TERRIBLE SHE BROKE DOWN CRYING ON THE BENCH. THE DOCTOR CHUCKLED, "I'M JUST SCREWING WITH YOU. HE'S DEAD. WHAT DID YOU SHOOT?"

Chapter 15

Golf is a Game of Ups and Downs: What is a Handicap?

HOLE HANDICAP

Before you read another word let me warn you that this will be the hardest chapter to get through. But stay with me and you will find out everything you ever wanted to know about handicaps but were smart enough not to ask about until now. The method by which the golf gods calculate handicaps requires an advanced degree in calculus. You may want to know the method to their madness. You may just want to know the bottom line. If you are a bottom-line kind of man or woman, I am going to give you the info in a nutshell — but I'm also going to give you the long-version, in–depth explanation as well. If you are a math wizard, you are going to love this chapter.

The handicap system is one of the unique features of golf. It allows the less-experienced players to be competitive against better players, both in a tournament format and a group match. There are two different kinds of "handicaps" in golf. One is an individual player's handicap (and it is more accurate to describe it as a "handicap index") and the other is the handicap rating of each individual golf hole on the course. They are different but intertwined. First cousins, once removed.

The hole handicap is easy: On an eighteen-hole golf course, each hole is evaluated for difficulty and assigned a number from 1 to 18, with 1 being the most difficult hole and 18 being the easiest. Pretty simple. So now let's complicate it a bit. In actuality, each of the eighteen holes is not compared to all the others on the course, but rather the front nine and the back nine are evaluated and compared separately. So the nine holes on the front nine are ranked from hardest to easiest, and the nine holes on the back nine are ranked from hardest to easiest. As a general rule, the front nine is ranked with odd numbers and the back nine with even numbers. So the hardest hole on the front nine would be ranked 1 and the easiest hole on the front nine would be ranked 17. The back nine is ranked identically, with the hardest hole ranked 2 and the easiest ranked 18. Relatively simple, right?

Almost. Keep in mind that because each group of nine holes is ranked against itself, the hardest hole on the back nine could be more challenging than the hardest hole on the front nine. Since the second handicapped hole is only being compared to the other eight holes on the back nine, just because the hardest hole is assigned the number 2 doesn't mean it is easier than the hardest hole on the front nine, the first handicapped hole. Right? And, theoretically, even the second hardest hole on the back nine (the fourth handicapped hole) could be more difficult than the hardest hole on the front nine (once again, the first handicapped hole). That would just mean that the hardest two holes on the back nine are harder than the most challenging hole on the front nine.

BOTTOM LINE:

Instead of going through gyrations trying to figure out which hole is harder than another, just assume that the holes often (though not always) increase in difficulty from the first handicapped hole to the eighteenth.

So why do we care about this? Well, the handicap of each set of nine holes is significant because when a player gets strokes because of how his individual handicap compares to the individual handicap of the other players he's competing against, the strokes he gets are applied in order of the handicaps of the holes. So, if you get five strokes (don't worry — I'll explain how you get these strokes below), you would get one stroke on handicapped holes 1 through 5 — three strokes on the front nine, two on the back nine. This means that if your final score on one of those five holes is a 6, for purposes of the competition your score would be 5, because you are getting a one stroke reduction on that hole. Your final score, which is utilized to determine your handicap, is not affected by your getting a stroke on any hole; in other words, when calculating your individual handicap, those five strokes do not reduce your overall score for the round by that number. These strokes are just used to even the playing field in the group match (or a tournament, if that format utilizes an individual score rather than a team score).

Remember, we are assuming an eighteen-hole round in our discussion above. So if you get five strokes for the eighteen-hole round, you would get a stroke on 1, 2, 3, 4, and 5 -- three on the front and two on the back. Of course, this brings up an interesting point: If you are playing a nine-hole match, the pro shop will cut your strokes in half. So if your handicap entitles you to five strokes, and you are only playing a nine-hole match, you would get strokes on 1, 3, and 5 because you are not playing the back nine, thus only three strokes, not five. Likewise, if your match is just the nine holes on the back nine, you would only get strokes on 2 and 4, thus two instead of five.

BOTTOM LINE:

If you get five strokes, you get one stroke for each of the handicap holes 1 through 5, not a stroke whenever you want to apply it (or more than one stroke on any one particular hole).

Experts (the USGA rating team) decide which holes are the easiest and which are the hardest, so your group doesn't get to determine the order of difficulty. You may also think the par 5s would be the hardest holes on the course. This may be the case on some courses, but sometimes a long par 4 or an especially difficult par 3 will be a harder hole, thus a lower handicapped hole, than an easy par 5.

INDIVIDUAL HANDICAP INDEX

If you thought everything I said above was complicated, you are really in trouble now. Let's talk about your individual handicap. When we talk about individual handicap indexes the first word that will pop up is GHIN (pronounced like gin of gin and tonic fame, which you should drink lots of to get through this chapter). GHIN is an acronym for Golf Handicap and Information Network. The GHIN system is brought to you by the same people who rate your golf courses — the United States Golf Association. The GHIN system allows golf clubs and golfers to post their scores so that each individual's handicap index can be calculated and, lo and behold, a number comes out that is your individual handicap index number.

BOTTOM LINE, GUYS AND GALS:

You will post your score after any nine-hole or eighteen-hole round. You can post it yourself at your course clubhouse, give it to the pro to post, or go online to the GHIN Web site to post. Periodically, your state-affiliated golf association will tell you your current index. If it has a decimal (17.4), you round it up or down to the nearest whole number for an informal group match only. In tournament play, decimals will always apply.

First, a little history. You would think that the handicap system was born in the computer age. But you would be wrong. Actually, the handicap system has been developed and debated since the earliest years of the twentieth century. However, in the early 1980s the handicapping system was greatly improved with the introduction of a "slope rating" for golf courses, which refined establishing an individual's handicap index based on his score on a particular golf course. This makes sense, doesn't it? I mean how could a 95 on a local pitch-and-putt course be treated the same way as a 95 at Pebble Beach? So now it's not just *what* a golfer shoots but *where* he shoots it. And that is what begins to complicate things.

There are two aspects of course evaluation that affect how your score is adjusted for purposes of your handicap index: The slope rating and the course rating. Let's start with course rating. To determine the course rating, the USGA decides what the top 50 percent of scratch golfers (a scratch golfer being someone who is expected to shoot par or better) would shoot, on average, from a specific set of tees on that specific golf course. A USGA course rating of 74.8 from the blue tees means that if you take the score of all of the scratch golfers playing the course from the blue tees and take the average score of the top 50 percent of them, that number would be 74.8. Theoretically, of course.

BOTTOM LINE:

The course rating from each set of tees (and the rating can be different for each tee) is the average score of the top half of pro (or scratch) golfers. Of course, the rating for the tips will be higher than the course rating for the forward tees. So a rating in the 70s indicates a more challenging course, because that means most scratch golfers will shoot par or higher. A rating in the 60s suggests an easier course, because that means the golfers will routinely shoot below par. A rating in the 50s? A miniature golf course!

The slope rating for a course is a number representing the relative difficulty of a course for bogey golfers compared to the course rating (which, as you know, is determined by scores of scratch golfers). Sounds easy enough, but hang onto your golf hat. In addition to establishing the course rating, the USGA rating team determines a "bogey rating" for the course. This is just what it sounds like: How many strokes a bogey golfer will take during his round. But then the USGA determines the difficulty of the course for bogey golfers relative to the difficulty of the course for scratch golfers. How? you may wonder. I'm glad you asked. To determine the slope of the course, the USGA takes the bogey-course rating minus the scratch-golfer rating (which is THE course rating) and multiplies it by 5.381 for men and 4.24 for women. Voilà. Slope rating.

PETE DYE'S OCEAN COURSE AT KIAWAH ISLAND IS RATED AS AMERICA'S MOST DIFFICULT GOLF COURSE BY **GOLF DIGEST.** *IT MEASURES 7,356 YARDS AND HAS THE HIGHEST COMBINATION OF SLOPE RATING (155) AND COURSE RATING (79.6) IN THE UNITED STATES.*

BOTTOM LINE:

The slope rating is always a number between 55 and 155, the "average" rating being 114. A slope rating in the 140s is very challenging; in the 130s, nothing to scoff at; in the 120s, challenging, but fun; in the 110s, average; below 110, pitch and putt.

And if you understood all that, let me add some more complications into these definitions. The USGA can't assign numbers to scratch or bogey golfers without having a way to determine what makes a golfer scratch (besides poison ivy) or a bogey player. So the USGA defines a scratch golfer as a male who hits his drive 250 yards and can reach a 470-yard hole in two, and typically shoots par or better; or a female golfer who hits her drives 210 yards and can reach a 400-yard hole in two. A bogey golfer is defined as a male with a handicap index of 17.5 to 22.4, who hits his drives 200 yards and can reach a 370-yard hole in two; and a female golfer with a handicap index of 21.5 to 26.4, who hits her drives 150 yards and can reach a 280-yard hole in two.

BOTTOM LINE:

If you hit your drive a long way and you usually shoot par you are a scratch golfer; if you hit your ball an average distance and your handicap is in the high teens for men or lower twenties for women, you are a bogey golfer. I am not a scratch golfer. I am barely a bogey golfer, although I would certainly be a bogey golfer if I were a woman.

That wasn't so bad, was it? Well, actually, that wasn't the hard part. This is: So the USGA determines the course and slope rating. *What does all of that have to do with us?* As I mentioned above, a 95 on a pitch-and-putt course cannot be treated the same way as a 95 on the Ko'olau golf course. Your individual official USGA Handicap Index is derived from a formula (nope, put that pen and paper away, I am not going to try to explain this formula, even if I knew how to do so) that takes into account adjusted gross score, course rating, and slope rating. What happens is that you play a round of golf at Shamrock Golf Course in Slippery Rock, Pennsylvania. You shoot a 98. Good for you. Now go to the GHIN Web site (or if computers are just too scary for you, let your golf pro do it). You type in your GHIN number (which you can get from your private club or, typically, you can buy for a modest fee from any public course) and the computer asks you when you played, where you played, what tees you played from, if it is your home course or an away course, if it was tournament play or regular play and, finally, what your damn score was. You have now posted your score. The computer program will then assign a number to that score adjusted by all the things mentioned above (so a 95 on a really hard course is worth more than a 95 on a really easy course) and it becomes part of your scoring history. Nope, not done yet.

THE KO'OLAU GOLF CLUB ON OAHU, HAWAII, USED TO HAVE A SLOPE RATING OF 162, BUT SINCE I ALREADY SAID PETE DYE'S OCEAN COURSE SLOPE RATING WAS THE HIGHEST AT 155 (SEE P. 171) AND KO'OLAU DIDN'T WANT TO MAKE A LIAR OF ME BY SAYING THEIR SLOPE RATING BEATS PETE'S, THEIR CURRENT SLOPE RATING IS 152.

With as few as five rounds you can get a handicap index assigned to you. However, until you have posted twenty scores your index is really not an index yet. Why? you ask. Thank you for asking. Your individual handicap index is ultimately calculated by using the best ten of your twenty most recent rounds. So the program takes your ten best scores after they have been adjusted by course rating and slope rating and a number comes out. Let's call it 17.4. Congratulations. That, my friend, is your USGA Handicap Index. Are we done yet? Nope, not yet. Why does the GHIN system care if you played at home or away? Because you are expected to play better on your home course than away at a course where you had no idea there was a hazard right before the green on hole number 11. So your score is weighted accordingly. And why does the GHIN system care if you are playing in a tournament or just for fun? Because you are expected to play better in a tournament, where you may actually be concentrating on your round instead of how much value your 401(k) lost in the last economic downturn. So how does a tournament score get weighted? The GHIN system compares the best ten of your last twenty rounds with your two best tournament scores recorded within the past twelve months. Not only does it compare them, it examines the gap between the best "ten of twenty" figure and the two lowest tournament scores. If your tournament scores are sufficiently low, additional calculations are made that factor in the size of the gap and it will lower your handicap index. (And if you never play in a tournament, don't worry; the GHIN system simply skips this calculation.)

> **BOTTOM LINE:**
> *Take your handicap index number and run.*

Now that you know your index is 17.4, does that mean you are going to shoot seventeen or eighteen shots above whatever is par for the course? No. First, because your handicap index utilizes your best ten scores out of the last twenty scores instead of your average ten scores out of the last twenty scores, your index represents your potential ability, not your actual ability.

And that's not all. Your individual handicap index can be adjusted at each course you play. That's right. Just as a 95 at an easy course is not the same as a 95 on a hard course, your index of 17.4 may not give you enough strokes on a difficult course and may give you too many strokes on a course that has windmills instead of hazards. Follow me here. If the course rating is 67.8, the top 50 percent of scratch golfers would have an average score of 67.8 (let's call it 68) on that course. On a harder course, the course rating is 71. The scratch golfer's score would be approximately three strokes higher on that course than on the easier course. The problem is that on a more challenging course, the average golfer may not just score three strokes higher than on the simpler course. Because he is average, the harder the course the harder it is for him JUST to score three strokes higher. So each course can adjust your index based on the difficulty of the course. If my index is 17 and I play on a really demanding course, my index on that course may be 21. At the same time, a golfer whose index is 2 may have his index adjusted by only one stroke, to a 3, because as a scratch golfer the difficulty of the course will not affect him as much as it affects me. Got it?

BOTTOM LINE:
Go into the pro shop, tell them your index, and ask them what your handicap is on their course.

NOW are we done? Nope, not yet. How do these numbers apply to our round of golf? Since the individual handicap index is used to equalize the playing field, if you are playing a match with your three pals, and your index is 17.4, you simply compare it to the indexes of everyone else in your foursome and you can come up with a fair number of strokes to give the three players with higher handicaps than the best player in the foursome. If, for example, the best player has an index of 10.2, you would "play off" of his index (17.4 - 10.2 rounded to the nearest whole number, of course) and get seven strokes. So you would get one stroke on handicap holes 1 through 7. You would do the same with the two other members of the foursome.

I really don't want to complicate this anymore, but it behooves me to mention that since a handicap index determines your best "potential" rather than your actual score, comparing your index with a player who does not have an index (and is just estimating his "average score") is really not fair to you. In such a situation, if a player says he usually shoots a 92, I would subtract par (the standard par value for a championship golf course is 72) from that average score (92 – 72 = 20) and then subtract three more strokes to adjust for your index (20 – 3 = 17). I would "assign" him an index of 17 based on the above equations for purposes of giving strokes.

So NOW are we done? Almost. Two paragraphs up, we rounded the difference between 17.4 and 10.2 to 7, because what were we going to do with the extra .2? Well the .2 could make a difference in a big field if there is a tie between individuals or teams. With an informal match amongst your foursome, a tie is unlikely, so .2 probably won't make a difference. But in a tournament with a big field, that extra .2 could be very important in breaking a tie. More about that in the next chapter.

Yea! We're finally done? Actually, not quite. But this will be the last word on handicaps in this chapter, I promise. Remember at the very beginning of the chapter I told you that you could post your score on the clubhouse computer, on the Internet, or give it to the pro to do for you? Well, that is true. But what I didn't tell you is *what* score to post. Does that sound provocative? No, it just sounds like the Equitable Stroke Control. The whatsy?

The ESC (and no, that's not that escape key on the computer you wish you had hit about ten paragraphs ago) is designed to "cap" the amount of strokes you can take on any particular hole so that a particularly bad hole does not skew your score. Okay, follow me here. In the movie *Tin Cup,* Kevin Costner knows he can hit his 3-wood onto the green in two and win the U.S. Open. He is so sure he can do that, he keeps trying the shot...over and over again. Unfortunately, his ball repeatedly keeps rolling back into the water after falling short of the green. So, let's say Kevin was shooting par before that and after all his shots and penalties he ends up with a 16 on the eighteenth hole. Instead of shooting a 72 he shoots an 83. Well, that is certainly going to affect his handicap, isn't it? Because the handicap calculations are based on twenty scores, when you post a new round the oldest score drops off. Therefore, even if that 83 is not one of his ten best scores, it may eliminate a score that was low and was utilized for his handicap. In short, an unusually bad score is going to affect a golfer's handicap one way or the other. What does the USGA do about situations like this? Easy, the ESC!

THE INTERNATIONAL (PINES) COURSE IN BOLTON, MASSACHUSETTS, WITH ITS 8,325 YARDS FROM THE TIPS, HAS A COURSE RATING OF 80 AND A SLOPE RATING OF 154.

The ESC tells you the maximum number of strokes you are allowed to take on a given hole on a given golf course. It is not based on your index but, rather, your index at the course on which you are playing (now do you see why I bothered explaining the course adjustment to you six paragraphs ago? There is always a purpose to my madness). So you find out what your handicap is on the course you are playing that day, and that will tell you the maximum number of strokes you are allowed to score (for purposes of your handicap) on a given hole. Remember, you can mark down that you got a 16 on a particular hole. You just can't count all those strokes in your final score when posting it to calculate your handicap.

If your course handicap index is 9 or less, the maximum number of strokes you can take for purposes of your handicap is a double bogey (two over par for each hole). If your course handicap index is 10 to 19, the maximum number of strokes per hole is seven (it doesn't matter if you are playing a par 3 or a par 5 — the most strokes you can count are 7). If your course handicap index is 20 to 29, the maximum number of strokes you can count is eight; If your course handicap index is 30 to 39, your maximum number of strokes is nine, and if your handicap index is 40 or more, your maximum count is ten. So if your handicap is 22 and it takes you ten strokes to finish that par 5, the most strokes you can count on that hole is eight. That is your score for your handicap calculation whether you actually get an 8 or a 20 on that hole.

Don't worry if you didn't find out about your ESC before you teed off: Hopefully, you will not have more than one or two disastrous holes in a round, so you can determine your adjustment before you post your score. One other nifty thing about the ESC is that it promotes a good pace of play, as discussed in chapter thirteen. Remember I told you that if you are hitting your tenth shot on the fairway of a par 4 you should probably just pick up your ball and start playing again on the next tee? You were worried that that would make the posting of your score dishonest, weren't you? Good for you. I like honest golfers. But you don't have to worry about it. Just put a big X on your scorecard, because there is a maximum number of strokes you can count for any hole, even if you don't finish the hole.

ARE WE FINALLY DONE WITH THIS CHAPTER ON HANDICAPS???
BOTTOM LINE: *Yes we are.*

A JOKE TO TELL WHILE YOU'RE CHOOSING UP TEAMS.

JOE WAS GETTING ON IN YEARS AND AFTER ONE PARTICULARLY FRUSTRATING ROUND HE CAME HOME VERY DISCOURAGED.

"WHAT'S THE PROBLEM, JOE?" HIS WIFE, JUDY, ASKED. "DIDN'T YOU HAVE A GOOD TIME PLAYING GOLF?"

"WELL I WAS HITTING THE BALL OKAY," JOE ANSWERED, "BUT MY EYESIGHT HAS GOTTEN SO BAD I COULDN'T FIND HALF MY BALLS."

"WELL, WHY DON'T YOU BRING YOUR BROTHER ALONG NEXT TIME YOU PLAY?" JUDY ASKED.

"FRED'S EIGHTY-FIVE YEAR'S OLD!" JOE ANSWERED. "HE DOESN'T EVEN PLAY GOLF ANYMORE."

"BUT HE'S GOT PERFECT EYESIGHT. HE DOESN'T HAVE TO PLAY GOLF TO WATCH YOUR BALL, DOES HE?" JUDY ANSWERED.

SO THE NEXT DAY JOE TOOK OFF FOR A ROUND OF GOLF WITH FRED. ON THE FIRST TEE, THE BALL TOOK OFF AND DISAPPEARED DOWN THE MIDDLE OF THE FAIRWAY. "DID YOU SEE IT?" JOE ASKED.

"OF COURSE," FRED ANSWERED.

"WELL, WHERE DID IT GO?" JOE ASKED, PEERING INTO THE DISTANCE.

"I FORGOT."

Chapter 16

Wanna Bet? Golf Tournament Formats and Group-Betting Games

GOLF TOURNAMENT FORMATS

Golf really gets to be fun when you start playing with other people — whether you know them or not — in a tournament. Virtually all golf courses have regular tournaments throughout the year. Some tournaments stretch an entire season and crown individual champions, some are simply one-day events that match one team against another.

Team tournaments are a great way of getting to meet new people or instill a sense of cooperation in a team event. Since most formats adjust scores based on individual handicaps, a beginning golfer can have as much fun in a tournament as a scratch golfer.

MATCH PLAY, STROKE PLAY

First, let's talk about the difference between match play and stroke play: In match play, scoring is accomplished on a hole-by-hole basis. Therefore, an individual or a team wins or loses each individual hole rather than accumulating a score over nine or eighteen holes. If a team has one really disastrous hole, they only lose that hole and not the entire match.

If you are competing against a different person each round each week, you get your handicap applied to your score, your opponent gets his handicap applied to his score, and you compete on each hole you play. So let's say on hole number 1 you get a stroke and your opponent does not. You both get a 5 on the hole. You win the hole because with your stroke applied to your score you end up with a 4. You get one point. On hole number 2, you get another stroke, but your score is an 8 compared to your opponent's 5. Even with one stroke you don't win the hole. But it doesn't matter if you get an 8 or an 18 on that hole, you only lose one hole. After nine holes (if you are playing a nine-hole match) you add up how many holes you won and how many holes your opponent won and whoever won more holes wins the match.

What if you both get the same score on a hole? No blood. So what if the final nine-hole match score is four holes won, four holes lost, and one tie? Typically, you go to the lowest handicapped hole for those nine holes and whoever won that hole wins the tie-breaker. If that hole (the first handicapped hole) was the hole that you tied, you would go to the next handicapped hole to determine the winner.

Stroke play is just the opposite: Accumulated scores are utilized over a certain number of holes, typically the entire round. On some matches you get 100 percent of your handicap applied. So, if you are playing in the club championship and you get your full handicap applied in stroke play, determining the winner is simple: You have a handicap of 17, you shoot a 94, your net score is 77. If an opponent has a handicap of 5, but shoots an 86, his net score is 81 and you win. Congratulations!

APPLYING HANDICAPS

You can get individual strokes applied to your score if you are playing an individual match against one other person or against a field of individuals golfers. There are also team competitions in which individuals receive strokes ("best ball," described later in this chapter). And sometimes you get a certain number of strokes for your entire team. In a team event such as a "scramble," when each member of the team hits his or her drive, then the team picks out the best hit, and takes their second shot from the site where the best ball landed — the tournament director would utilize a team handicap.

How do handicaps work in team competition? Well, it is possible that no team gets a handicap: Every team just competes against every other team, and the team with the best score in the end wins. However, if handicaps are not applied and one team member is a scratch golfer, that team has a very good chance of beating the rest of the field. Of course, if you don't have a ringer on your team it's not quite as much fun.

The course can also establish "flighted" teams rather than applying individual handicaps. This means that the field is equally divided into four different skill levels (flights A, B, C, and D), and each team has a person from each flight, thus, presumably equalizing the talent. This levels the playing field, but such assignments — based on degrees of proficiency — typically result in players being grouped where needed and not necessarily being able to choose their own team or play with their friends.

A tournament that *does* let golfers choose their own teammates runs the risk of being imbalanced, where one team is so good that the rest of the field doesn't have a chance of winning. Thus, the way to equalize the teams and make them more competitive is to add up everyone's handicaps and then give each team a percentage of strokes off their final score based on this team handicap total. For example, if a team of four has handicaps of 4, 14, 15, and 23, the total team handicap is 56. The tournament director would then take a percentage – 10, 15, or even 25 percent – of the team handicap to determine the team handicap. So let's say he gives each team 15 percent of their handicap. That means that the team's final score will be reduced by 8.4 strokes (15 percent of 56). If the best team in the field has handicaps of 2, 4, 4, and 8, and they receive 15 percent of their team handicap, they would receive 2.7 strokes off their final score (15 percent of 18). If the 56-handicapped team ends up with a team score of 68, their "net" score would be 59.6 (68 minus 8.4). If the 18-handicapped team ends up with a team score of 65, their net score is 62.3 (65 minus 2.7) and the higher-handicapped team would win the event. Obviously, the higher the percentage applied to the team handicap, the better the chance the team with a higher handicap has of winning or placing in the tournament.

Some tournaments award places for best gross score and best net score. So the 56-handicapped team, which ended up with a net score of 59.6, would win first place net, but the 18-handicapped team, which ended up with a 65 before the handicap was applied, would win first place gross. Typically, a team would prefer to win in the gross division rather than the net division, but a win is a win! If a team has the best net score and the second-best gross score, they do not win both: The highest place is awarded first. So the team would be awarded the best net score. Depending on the size of the field, a tournament may award prizes for as many as four or five places, both gross and net.

Hole	1	2	3	4	5	6	7	8	9	Out	10	11	12	13	14	15	16	17	18	In	Tot	Hcp	Net
Black 74.2/145	391	349	568	430	203	560	213	421	380	3515	336	507	359	176	395	559	350	215	436	3333	6848		
Blue 72.0/140	367	337	537	414	155	538	181	393	369	3291	328	490	349	148	367	527	326	191	401	3127	6418		
Member 71.2/138	363	308	511	409	137	538	156/188	393/356	360	3175/3170	321	445	331	148	367	527	326	166	401	3032	6207/6202		
White M 69.9/134 W 76.1/137	358	308	511	402	137	498	156	365	327	3062	321	445	331	138	361	503	301	166	391	2957	6019		
Men's Hcp	9	15	3	1	17	5	11/7	7/11	13		8	10	12	18	6	2	14	16	4				
Ken	5	7	7	6	4	7	4	5	7														
Rob	5	5	6	7	5	6	4	4	4														
+/-	+1	–	-1	–	+1	–	+1	+1	–														
Tiebreaker – #4 – 6' < 7' = Win																							
Par	4	4	5	4	3	5	3	4	4	36	4	5	4	3	4	5	4	3	4	36	72		
Red 70.8/121	328	281	468	303	135	450	116	287	309	2677	257	380	271	101	291	416	231	121	302	2370	5047		
Gold M 68.4/131 W 74.2/129	328	308	468	303	155	498	156	287	327	2830	321	445	331	138	291	503	301	166	350	2846	5676		
Women's Hcp	7	13	1	5	17	3	15	9	11		10	6	12	18	8	2	14	16	4				

DATE: ______ SCORER: ______ ATTEST: ______

A scorecard reflecting a two-person, nine-hole match (won by the better score on the first handicapped hole, number 4).

What happens if two teams (or more) have the same gross or net score? As described above, the tournament director goes to the hardest hole on the course (the number-one handicap hole) to see who got the best score on that hole, continuing to the second, third, and other handicap holes down the line until he gets to the hole where one team had a lower score than the other, or he'll simply start on the first hole and go in numerical order until he reaches the hole where one team had a lower score than the other. Because it is likely the pro will start with the lowest-handicapped holes to determine a winner, those are the holes on which you want to take special care to do your best (and to use any special gimmicks, described below, to enhance your score).

TOURNAMENT FORMATS

Now on to the most common tournament formats. Unless stated otherwise, individual handicaps typically apply in individual tournament formats and team handicaps are applied in team versus team competition.

1. The Scramble — As described earlier in this chapter, this is by far the most common tournament format you will find for team competition. Although a scramble can be played by teams of two, three, or four (or some combination of the three), it is more typical to have four players to a team. The basic premise of a scramble is that every player hits his individual ball and then the team chooses the best ball of the four and everyone hits their second shot from the ball they chose as the best ball. This continues until the ball is in the hole. There is one score for the team and it is very common for the team score to be a birdie, par, or no worse than a bogey. Obviously, a scramble utilizes the stroke-play scoring system because it is the final score of EACH TEAM that is compared, not each individual hole.

If one team only has three players, typically each player takes turns hitting the fourth shot on alternating holes. So player number one would hit twice on hole number 1, 4, 7, etc., and player number two would hit the extra shot on hole number 2, 5, 8, etc. With a three-person team, the handicap is determined by simply taking the average of the three players and multiplying it by four; if the three players have handicaps of 13, 17, and 21, the total of the three is 51, the average is 17, and the team handicap before a pecentage is applied is 68 (17 multiplied by 4). This is logical since the three-player team gets four hits of every ball just like a four-person team.

You will also often hear that the tournament will have a "shotgun" start. This doesn't mean you hit the ball with a shotgun instead of a golf club.

It means that every team goes to an assigned hole to start their round and they all begin at the same time. This results in all teams ending their round at approximately the same time; if a team starts on hole number 5, then after completing hole number 18 they would simply play holes 1 through 4 as their final four holes.

A tournament can also utilize starting times for each team. But that would stretch a tournament out as long as it takes for every team to tee off from hole number 1.

2. The Texas Scramble — This is a variation on a straight scramble in which every player must contribute four drives to the round of golf. This eliminates the team using the best player's drive every time. A tournament director can require each team to use a set number of drives by each player, but a Texas Scramble is specifically four.

3. The Florida Scramble — In this variation, once the preferred ball is selected, whoever hit that shot does not get to hit the next shot. The second shot would be hit by only three players (the player who hit the selected shot sitting out the second shot), the third by only two players, and the fourth by only one player.

4. Best Ball — In this tournament, all members of each team play their own balls on each hole. At the completion of the hole, the lowest score among all team members serves as the team score. Each player utilizes his own individual handicap on each hole. So if your handicap is 20, you would receive one stroke on every hole plus a second stroke on the first and second handicap holes. If, with your handicap, you have the lowest score, then that becomes the team score for the hole. A variation of this format is Two Best Ball, in which the two best scores on a team of four are utilized to determine the team's score on every hole.

5. Two Person Best Ball — Just a variation of Best Ball, but teams consist of two golfers rather than three or four. Same rules apply. This format is often used in private-club tournaments.

6. 1-2-3 Best Ball — Yet another variation of Best Ball played with four-person teams. On the first hole, only the best score is utilized. On the second hole, the lowest two scores are used, and on the third hole, the lowest three scores are counted. No, the fourth hole does not use all four scores: It goes back to the one best score and progresses as described above through the remainder of the holes.

7. Alternate Shot — The Alternate Shot format is for two-person teams. The two players on each team take turns hitting one ball. So Player A would drive on hole 1, Player B would hit the second shot no matter where the first shot landed, etc.

8. Stableford — The Stableford format is an individual competition. The winner of a Stableford tourney would be the golfer who gets the highest number of points in relation to a fixed score at each hole. For example, let's say the club has established the fixed score of 6 for each hole. If you get more than one over that fixed number (an 8 or more), you would not get any points. If you get a 7 (one over the fixed number), you get one point. If you get a 6, you get two points; 5, three points; 4, four points, etc. The player with the most points wins. You can play in a foursome, but it is an individual tournament in that each player is playing against everyone else in the field. Note that the fixed number is THE number on each hole, no matter what the par is for each individual hole.

Individual handicaps should be applied as logic dictates. If you get eleven strokes, you would get one stroke on the first eleven handicapped holes. After your handicap is applied for each hole, the points are assigned as described above. Therefore, if the fixed number is 6 and you get a 7, but you get a stroke on that hole, you end up with a 6 and the two points you get for hitting the fixed number.

9. Modified Stableford — A Modified Stableford tournament is a Stableford tournament that has been modified (just seeing if you're paying attention). Actually, the Modified Stableford is more common than the Stableford tourney. Rather than set a fixed number for each hole, the points a golfer gets are determined by how much over or under par he ends up on the hole. A double bogey or worse would cause you to lose three points, a bogey would cause you to lose one point, a par zero points, a birdie gets you plus two points, an eagle five points, and a double eagle eight points. Handicaps are applied for each individual hole before points are assigned. The player with the highest score wins the individual tourney.

10. The Chapman or Pinehurst — The Chapman or Pinehurst format is a combination of various formats described above. It is typically limited to two-person teams in which each of the two players switches balls after the other drives a ball; after their second shot they pick the Best Ball (as in a Scramble), and then play alternate shots until the ball is in the hole.

11. Flags — In a Flags tournament all golfers begin the round with a set number of strokes (calculated using their handicap), and they play until their strokes run out. The player who makes it the farthest into his or her round wins the tournament (when you use all of your allotted strokes you put your flag in the ground and go have a beer until everyone finishes their round).

12. Lone Ranger — Also called Money Ball, Yellow Ball, or Pink Ball, each player takes a turn (in a pre-assigned rotation) on each hole to have their score count. So in a group of four, Player A is the Lone Ranger on the first hole and only his score counts; Player B is the Lone Ranger on the second hole and only her score counts, etc. The score of the designated Lone Ranger is combined with the low score of the other three team members for a two-score team score. So if on the first hole, the Lone Ranger gets a 6 and among the other three players the best score is a 4, the total team score for the hole is 10.

13. Twilight leagues — A twilight league is not a tournament format, but is similar to a bowling league in that members of the course or club compete against one another on a selected weekday afternoon for a set period of time (typically five to eight weeks) in whatever format is deemed desirable by the club (straight match-play, straight stroke-play, Stableford, etc.). Typically, a twilight league will pit two individuals of similar playing skill against each other in a match-play format for nine holes, which means there may be six or more flighted "groups" competing within their own bracket (if there are forty-eight players, the pro will form six groups of eight players, putting the best eight players in Bracket A, the next eight players in Bracket B, etc.). Each player plays against the other golfers in their bracket (with handicaps applied, of course), and the individual who wins the most matches against the others in their bracket wins the competition (yeah!).

A club can use the Stableford or Modified Stableford format if it prefers everyone in the bracket to compete individually every week rather than in a series of two-person matches. It is up to each individual club to decide which format to utilize. The bottom line is that this is a great way to get golfers out on a regular basis, to fill up a slow afternoon (league play is often on a Tuesday, Wednesday, or Thursday afternoon, normally slow periods for golf courses), and introduces solo golfers to other members of the club.

Twilight leagues are a great opportunity for the beginning golfer to meet other players at the same level of skill, to learn how to play golf with the pressure of competition (see why I told you to not always accept a gimmie putt, just in case, someday, you have to make that six-inch putt to win a match?), and to learn how to play strictly by the rules (there are no gimmies or mulligans in tournament play — you play your ball from the tee shot until you hear your ball rolling in the cup. That's golf the way it is meant to be played). If your club has a twilight league (and it will typically have a separate men's and women's league and often have two or three leagues during the golf season), sign up and hone your game!

Now that you know the basic tournament formats, there are also fun "gimmicks" that can make any tournament or league even more entertaining.

A. Closest to the pin — A contest on a par 3, where you measure which drive of the entire field ends up closest to the pin. It is typical to have separate closest-to-the-pin contests for men and women on different par 3s.

B. Longest drive — This is usually a hole that is fairly long and as each succeeding "long drive" is hit, a place marker is moved forward for the new "leader." Typically, the drive has to be on the fairway to qualify for the longest drive and, as is true with closest to the hole, there is usually a longest drive for men and a separate one for women.

C. Straightest drive — This is a variation on the longest drive and you don't find it as often during a tournament. A white line is drawn down the fairway and the ball that lands closest to the line is awarded the "straightest drive." This can also be divided into fields for men and women.

D. Hole in one — It is very common, particularly in charity tournaments, that if you get a hole in one you can win anything from a set of golf clubs to a new car. The golf course can actually buy insurance just in case a player in a charity scramble event wins a car by hitting a hole in one.

E. One hole, one club — This is a hole on which everyone on the team can only play with a particular club (for example, on hole number 8 everyone has to use only their 9-iron). Often tournament directors will try to coordinate the hole with the club (typically, the 8-iron on the eighth hole or the 9-iron on the ninth hole).

In a charity tournament, you can often "buy" special gimmicks that can both make the tournament more fun and raise more money for the charity. These can include:

F. Hitting the green — This is different from the closest to the pin. You pay a nominal sum ($5.00) and if your drive lands on the green on the preselected par 3 you get a prize, often a sleeve of balls.

G. Casino hole — This is identical to hitting the green (above), except that prior to your round you buy into the pot, which can be $5.00 to $25.00, and anyone who hits the green on the casino hole with their drive enters a drawing to win half the pot (with the other half typically going to charity).

H. Mulligans — Some tournaments will let you buy up to two mulligans. A mulligan lets you take a second shot any time you wish. It's usually not "transferable" to another player, but it can be very useful when no one hits a decent drive or everyone misses that three-foot putt.

I. Golden tee — This is when you "buy" a tee, which allows you to tee up one shot on the fairway any time you want (usually a par 5 when you are trying to reach the green with a second shot).

J. The String — Prior to a tournament you can buy a certain number of strings without knowing the length of the strings you have bought until after they have been purchased (the length is hidden on the side of the table where the person collecting money is sitting). The strings can be used to move a ball the length of the string without counting it as another stroke. Strings are usually used on the green and allow you to count a missed putt as going into the hole. (For example, if you are twenty feet from the pin and your putt misses the hole by a foot, and one of the strings you purchased is a foot-and-a-half long, you can use the string to count your putt as having gone into the hole. Of course, the string can only be used one time.)

K. The Throw — This is another purchased stroke that buys you the right to pick up your ball and throw it instead of hitting it. Great if the best shot of your group in a scramble is in a sand trap.

GROUP-BETTING GAMES

Once you get into the rhythm of playing with your pals, someone in your group is going to suggest playing an informal match. It is true that playing a match can make a game more interesting and make a player pay more attention to what he is doing. It can also put a lot of pressure on the beginning golfer. Don't hesitate to play a match if you feel comfortable doing so and you think you won't feel bad if you don't win. On the other hand, don't play a match if you don't want to or if you feel the wager is out of proportion to your skill level or what you are willing to lose. The good news is that most groups rarely play a match that results in a loss of more than twenty dollars. And there are matches for two or three players, so your participation is not required for others to be able to play a match.

CHOOSING TEAMS

Just as is true in tournaments, some group matches are individual and some involve teams. There are several ways to select teams. The individual with the highest handicap can be the partner of the player with the lowest handicap. You can throw all four balls into the air and the two closest to one side of the toss play against the two closest to the other side. Or after everyone hits his or her drive on the first hole, the longest driver can partner with the shortest driver.

GETTING STROKES

Just as is true in tournament formats, you need to even the playing field in an informal group match by applying handicaps. You don't have to go crazy and find out from the pro shop your adjusted handicap based on the course and your index. But you need to ascertain a reasonable handicap for each player and give strokes to each player based on his or her comparative skill.

As mentioned earlier, in a tournament the number of strokes a player gets is theoretically his handicap; in a group match the three higher handicapped players simply "play off" the handicap of the lowest-handicapped player. For example, if the four golfers in a group have handicaps of 8, 14, 18, and 20, the player with the 8 handicap would get no strokes, the player with the 14 handicap would get six strokes (14 minus 8), the 18 handicapper would get ten strokes, and the 20 handicapper, even if he eventually teamed up with the 8 handicapper, would get twelve strokes. A GHIN handicap index, since it reflects your potential and not your actual ability, will be lower than simply subtracting the par for the course from a presumed average score. Therefore, it's appropriate to subtract par from your average score and subtract an additional two or three strokes to be fair to the player with an index. If your average score is 95, you would deduct 72 from 95 (if 72 is par for the course) and subtract three more strokes for a "handicap" of 20 (95 minus 72 minus 3). All this being said, since this is an informal match, the group can simply decide a "fair" number of strokes to assign each participant. It's negotiable.

THE LOWEST SCORE FOR 18 HOLES OF GOLF ON THE PGA TOUR IS 59. THIS FEAT HAS BEEN ACCOMPLISHED BY AL GEIBERGER (1977 MEMPHIS CLASSIC, COLONIAL COUNTRY CLUB, PAR 72); CHIP BECK (1991 LAS VEGAS INVITATIONAL, SUNRISE GOLF CLUB, PAR 72); AND DAVID DUVAL (1999 BOB HOPE CHRYSLER CLASSIC, PGA WEST, PALMER COURSE, PAR 72).

So how would strokes affect scores in a match? Let's say hole number 1 on the course is the seventh handicapped hole (meaning the seventh hardest hole on the course, the fourth hardest hole on the front nine). Neither Player A nor Player B gets a stroke on that hole because Player A doesn't get any strokes on any hole and Player B only gets a stroke on the hardest six holes. Players C and D do get a stroke because they get at least seven strokes each. So if Players A, B, and C all get a 5 on hole number 1, and Player D gets a 6 on that hole, who has the lowest score? Player C, because Players A and B, without a stroke, tie each other; Player D, with a stroke, ties Players A, B, and C; but Player C, with a stroke, ends up with a net final score of 4, one less than Players A, B, or D. So whatever team that Player C is on would "win" the first hole (assuming the group is playing a team match, as described below). If no one had won the hole (Player C got a 6 instead of a 5), there is "no blood," meaning no one wins that hole. Simple! And based on the description above, Players B, C, and D all get strokes on handicapped holes 1 through 6 (which, remember, are not the first six holes, but the six hardest holes as determined by the hole handicaps); Players C and D would also get strokes on handicapped holes 7 through 10; and Player D alone would get a stroke on handicapped holes 11 and 12.

The most common matches you will play in a typical round of golf include:

1. Nassau — This is probably the most frequently played group match. Team A plays against Team B for three different matches: One on the front nine, one on the back nine, and one for the entire eighteen holes. Typically, the bet is $2.00 to $5.00 for each of the three segments.

Since nine out of ten times if you play a match it will be a Nassau, let's walk through a typical round. On the first hole Player One on Team A shoots a 5. His teammate gets a stroke on that particular hole and he, too, gets a 5. However, with his one stroke, the 5 becomes a 4 and he has the best score of Team A. Let's say neither Player One nor Player Two on Team B get a stroke on hole number 1. If Player One gets a 5 and Player Two gets a 7, then the best score on Team B is a 5. Team A wins the hole with the best score of 4. One for the good guys!

On to the second tee. Let's say no one wins the second hole. Team A is still one hole up. If Team B wins hole number 3, both teams would now be even. If Team B wins holes number 4 and 5, they would now be "two up." If there is no blood on the remainder of the holes on the front nine, Team B would win the front nine by two holes and would now be leading for the eighteen-hole match by two holes (which means if Team A doesn't win the back nine by three or more holes, Team B would win the front nine and the eighteen, two of the three Nassau matches). Of course, that assumes that Team A did not "press" Team B when they were behind two holes by the fifth hole.

What? Did I say "press?" You may ask, "Does that mean Team A has to press the pants of the players on Team B just because they are losing by two holes?" No, of course not! (Although that would be a fun penalty to impose on the loser.) If you weren't particularly enamored of the chapter on handicaps, this is a good time to move on to the next group-betting game and let your partner score all matches. However, if you want to understand everything there is to know about golf, read on and bear with me.

A press is made when you are losing a match and you want to do a sort of "double or nothing" wager to give your team a chance to recover. When your team presses, you are starting a new bet within the original bet. There is no set rule to pressing. It is up to every group to define the terms of the new wager they want to make on that day. Okay, let's go back to the match we were playing above. Team B is up two after five holes. But you, Player One on Team A, are starting to feel that your team has mojo and can win most of the remaining four holes on the front nine. Time to "press your luck" and press Team B. "We're pressing you," you declare with great confidence! This means that the first bet continues, but a new bet is started for holes 6 through 9.

So, your confidence was well-founded, and you win holes 6 and 7. Good job! You have now tied the original bet (you each have won three holes and tied one) and you are up two on the new bet, the press. You can do no worse than tie the press, even if Team B wins holes 8 and 9, because that would be two holes each on the press. Of course, you would lose the original bet, because although winning holes 6 and 7 tied the score on the original bet, if you lose holes 8 and 9 (the original bet continues simultaneously with the press), you will have lost the original bet by two holes. But if you win either hole 8 or hole 9, you will win the press and you could win the original bet. If your team wins just one of the final two holes, you could either tie or lose the original bet. Let's score it both ways. If you win hole 8 and tie hole 9, you win the press, and you win the original bet, so now you've won four, lost three, and tied two. If you win hole 8 and lose hole 9, you will still win the press (three wins, one loss), but you will have tied the original bet with four wins each and one tied hole. Got it? Trust me, it's easier than it sounds. All you need to do is to start counting wins, losses, and ties on a second line when the press begins. It becomes clear as you do it.

"Er, wait a minute, Ken," you might say. "You pressed Team B when you were down two holes. Why didn't Team B press you back when you won the first two holes of the press (holes 6 and 7)?" Well, they can and probably did (we'll show you who is confident and who is a pretender). First, remember that Team B is not pressing Team A on the original bet, because the score is currently tied on that bet (you don't press unless you are losing). But because Team B is losing the *press* by two strokes, they can start a third bet for the final two holes on the front nine. If Team

B wins holes 8 and 9 (ouch, that didn't go so well, did it?) they would win the original bet (five holes to two holes to one tie). If Team B wins holes 8 and 9 (ouch, that didn't go so well, did it?) they would win the original bet (five holes to two holes to one tie). There would be no blood on the first press since Team A won holes 6 and 7, but Team B won holes 8 and 9. Team B would win the second press (because they won the last two holes). That's okay. No harm done. The end result is that Team B won two of the three matches on the front nine, which nets out to them winning one match, which would have happened without presses. Of course, Team B will be very unhappy if it loses the second press (holes 8 and 9). Yep, three bets lost and we haven't even started the back nine! Well, that's the life of a gambler. You live by the 9-iron, you die by the 9-iron.

See why I said this section was similar to the chapter on handicaps? And by the way, we're not done yet. The group can decide whether:

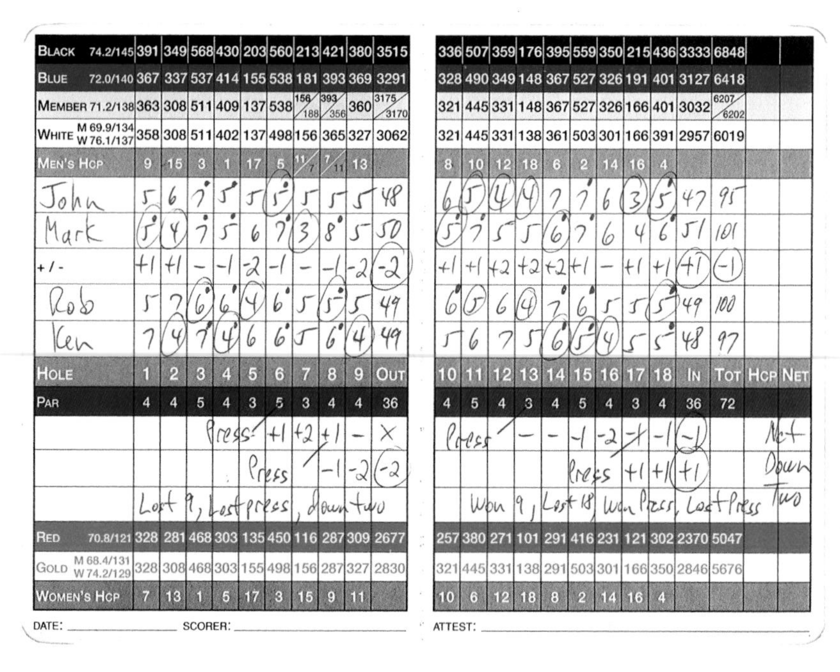

BLACK 74.2/145	391	349	568	430	203	560	213	421	380	3515	336	507	359	176	395	559	350	215	436	3333	6848		
BLUE 72.0/140	367	337	537	414	155	538	181	393	369	3291	328	490	349	148	367	527	326	191	401	3127	6418		
MEMBER 71.2/138	363	308	511	409	137	538	156/188	393/356	360	3175/3170	321	445	331	148	367	527	326	166	401	3032	6207/6202		
WHITE M 69.9/134 W 76.1/137	358	308	511	402	137	498	156	365	327	3062	321	445	331	138	361	503	301	166	391	2957	6019		
MEN'S HCP	9	15	3	1	17	5	11/7	7/11	13		8	10	12	18	6	2	14	16	4				
John	5	6	7	5	5	5	5	5	5	48	6	5	4	4	7	7	6	3	5	47	95		
Mark	5	4	7	5	6	7	3	8	5	50	5	7	5	5	6	7	6	4	6	51	101		
+/-	+1	+1	–	-1	-2	-1	–	-1	-2	-2	+1	+1	+2	+2	+2	+1	–	+1	+1	+1	-1		
Rob	5	7	6	6	4	6	5	5	5	49	6	5	6	4	7	6	5	5	5	49	100		
Ken	7	4	7	4	6	6	5	6	4	49	5	6	7	5	6	5	4	5	5	48	97		
HOLE	1	2	3	4	5	6	7	8	9	OUT	10	11	12	13	14	15	16	17	18	IN	TOT	HCP	NET
PAR	4	4	5	4	3	5	3	4	4	36	4	5	4	3	4	5	4	3	4	36	72		
			Press			+1	+2	+1	–	X	Press			–	–	-1	-2	-1	-1	-1			Net
					Press			-1	-2	-2						Press		+1	+1	+1			Down
	Lost 9, Lost press, down two										Won 9, Lost 18, Won Press, Lost Press												Two
RED 70.8/121	328	281	468	303	135	450	116	287	309	2677	257	380	271	101	291	416	231	121	302	2370	5047		
GOLD M 68.4/131 W 74.2/129	328	308	468	303	155	498	156	287	327	2830	321	445	331	138	291	503	301	166	350	2846	5676		
WOMEN'S HCP	7	13	1	5	17	3	15	9	11		10	6	12	18	8	2	14	16	4				

DATE: ________ SCORER: ________ ATTEST: ________

A four-person, two-team match in which Team A lost the front nine, the eighteen hole match, and two presses, but won the back nine and one press, for a net loss of two.

1) no presses are allowed, 2) the team ahead has to accept a press, 3) the team ahead can decline the press (cowards!), 4) you have to be losing by two holes to press, 5) a team that's two holes behind is required to press, 6) you cannot press on the ninth or eighteenth hole (the theory being that it is unfair to have a one-hole match to negate a two-hole deficit), 7) and they may ask *what is the meaning of life when you can't just go out and play a little golf without everything becoming so complicated?* Well, you get the idea. Maybe having your partner just keep score for you was the smart thing to do after all!

2. Round Robin — This is a variation of the Nassau played by a foursome. Each player plays one set of six holes with every other player. You can play a round robin with handicaps or without handicaps, because if everyone plays with everyone else, the presumption is that the skills even out. A round robin would have three different bets for each six holes.

3. Bingo Bango Bongo — This is a fun match for individual competition. A player receives one point for accomplishing one of three things on each hole: Being the first player in the group to get onto the green; or being closest to the hole once all group members are on the green for the first time (meaning not after one player putts); or being the first player in the cup after all group members are on the green (which requires honors being strictly followed, because if you are farthest from the hole you are entitled to the first opportunity to score the third point). In this format even the highest handicapper of the foursome can win, because he may be the last on the green, but could be the closest to the pin if his prior shot fell just short of the green.

4. Wolf — Wolf is a great game for a group of four, but it, too, can be complicated. Stick with me. Players rotate being the wolf (in an order that's determined prior to the start of the match). On each hole, the wolf gets to choose whether to play against all three other players in the group or to choose a partner and play two against two. If the wolf goes it alone and he gets the best score (after handicaps are applied), he wins three points. If he plays with a teammate and he and the teammate win the hole, each teammate gets one point. The game continues until the round is over and the person with the most points wins, whatever the wager is.

5. Skins — Skins is a match in which a value is assigned to each hole and whoever wins the hole wins the skin. So if the "skin" is $1.00, whoever wins the first hole wins a dollar from all of the other players, and so forth and so on for eighteen holes. There is no tie for a hole. If no one wins a hole, the skin just gets carried forward to the next hole, which would then be worth two dollars. Skins is probably the best game to play when your group is a threesome, because with a foursome ties are more frequent. Although the scoring of a skins game seems fairly straightforward, it's actually not, because some of the skins you win will be offset by the skins you lose. This is more complicated than it sounds (although nothing compared to pressing).

Let me show you the easiest way to settle up after a skins game. Let's assume a threesome and each skin is worth $1.00 a hole. Visualize the pot as if everyone threw in $18.00 at the beginning of the round, thus creating a total of $54.00. Let's assume there is no tie on the eighteenth hole, so every skin is won by someone. If everyone wins six skins, there is no blood and no money changes hands. The only other two mathematical possibilities are: 1) there's one winner and two losers, or 2) there are two winners and one loser. Let's score both.

You win nine skins (congratulations!), our pal (let's call him Mike) wins seven skins, and I win two skins. You win $27.00 ($9.00 multiplied by 3), which includes the dollars you threw into the pot). Since your "contribution" is a total of $18.00, you will end up netting $9.00 (consisting of the theoretical $18.00 you contributed, which is still in your pocket, and the $9.00 you won from the other players). The only issue is who has to pay you. Since Mike won seven skins, he gets $21.00, a net win of $3.00 ($21.00 minus his original $18.00). Since I only won two skins, I am going to owe you the $9.00 and Mike the $3.00. This works out mathematically because if I win two skins, I win $6.00, but with my investment of $18.00, my net loss is $12.00, which, lo and behold, equals the $9.00 plus $3.00 that I owe.

I paid you two. If Mike won five skins instead of seven, and I won the extra two skins instead of you, that would make you the only winner and Mike and I would both be losers. The math remains the same: You win $27.00, net $9.00, I win $12.00 instead of $6.00, resulting in a net loss of $6.00 instead of $12.00, and Mike owes the extra $3.00, because his five skins ($15.00) nets him a loss of $3.00. Easy, huh? Just take your skins, multiply by three (for a threesome, four for a foursome), subtract from $18.00 (if the bet is $1.00 a hole) or subtract $18.00 from your total if you win more than six holes, and the remaining players will owe you some money, which you can promptly spend on drinks for the group.

6. Madagascar — This is my favorite match of all time (and is intended to be a joke match). Each hole is worth $1,000.00, you play every gimmick described below, but no one pays anyone unless or until everyone meets someday in Madagascar. Just make sure you don't mention your travel plans to your opponents in the future if you happen to lose by six or seven holes!

Besides matches between or among the players, the group can also have side bets for individual "achievements." All these have a value set at the beginning of the round, which is typically when each player is called on to give the achiever a dollar for each accomplishment. Although you can play these as team bets (in other words, if one member of the two-man team wins the side bet the team divides the spoils), it is probably more fun to play these wagers as individual achievements independent of the team match. Here are seven examples:

7. Greenies — A greenie is a side bet that only applies on the par 3s. After everyone hits their drive, the ball closest to the pin (but only if it lands on the green on the drive) wins the bet from the other players. The way most groups play (and make sure your group agrees on this rule *before* the first person hits) is that not only must a golfer's ball be closest to the pin, but that he must make the par to win the bet. This one will really put the pressure on you.

8. Sandy — A sandy is when a player makes par on a hole in which he was in a green-side sand trap. You can also agree that a sandy can be won if a player is in a fairway bunker and makes par. Whichever or both, agree before you start playing.

9. Barkie — A barkie is when a player makes a par after solidly hitting a tree on the hole.

10. Stickie — A stickie is when a player hits the flagstick and it goes into the hole.

11. Poley — A poley is when a player is on the green in regulation (two strokes less than par) and, before he starts putting, his ball is flagstick-distance from the pin.

12. Arnie — An Arnie is when a player makes a par without ever having been on the fairway. Named in honor of Arnold Palmer, who made quite a few "Arnies" in his time.

13. The Snake — This will improve your putting considerably. The first person who 3-putts a hole "owns" the snake and keeps it until someone else 3-putts a green (if the snake owner and someone else both 3-putt the same hole, the snake owner gets to keep the snake). Whoever has the snake after the final hole owes each player $1.00.

A JOKE TO TELL WHILE YOU'RE BUYING THAT POWER BAR FROM THE REFRESHMENT CART.

A THREESOME OF A FATHER AND TWO SONS WAS ABOUT TO TEE OFF WHEN THE PRO APPROACHED THE GROUP WITH A BEAUTIFUL WOMAN GOLFER AND SAID, "GENTLEMEN, REBECCA IS LOOKING FOR A GROUP TO PLAY WITH. WOULD YOU MIND IF SHE JOINED YOU TODAY?"

REBECCA WAS WELCOMED INTO THE GROUP AND IT TURNED OUT SHE WAS AS TALENTED A GOLFER AS SHE WAS BEAUTIFUL. THE GROUP FINALLY ARRIVED AT THE EIGHTEENTH GREEN AND REBECCA'S BALL WAS ABOUT TEN FEET FROM THE PIN. REBECCA TURNED TO THE THREE MEN AND SAID, "LISTEN, GUYS, THIS IS THE BEST ROUND I HAVE EVER PLAYED. IF I SINK THIS PUTT I WILL BREAK 80 FOR THE FIRST TIME. WHOEVER CAN GIVE ME THE BEST READ ON THIS PUTT I WILL TREAT TO A STEAK DINNER AND A NIGHT ON THE TOWN."

THE FIRST SON SAID, "REBECCA, THIS IS EASY. I SEE A SIX-INCH BREAK TO THE LEFT."

THE SECOND SON SAID, "ABSOLUTELY NOT. THE HOLE IS SLOPING TOWARD THE WATER. AIM ABOUT TWO INCHES TO THE LEFT AND IT SHOULD FALL RIGHT IN."

THE FATHER THOUGHT A MINUTE AND SAID, "I'LL GIVE YOU THE PUTT."

Chapter 17

Miss a Putt but Not This Information (Everything Else You Need to Know)

Golf is full of smaller nuances that do not fit nicely into a category. Let's call this a catchall of the final tidbits of information you need before you head out for your next round of golf.

THE TRAVELING GOLFER

There is nothing more exciting to me than going on vacation or a business trip and being able to play golf at a course I have never seen before (or, better yet, a course I've heard of many times and have always wanted to play).

The first question you ask yourself is, *Should I bring my own clubs or rent clubs at the course?* First, you should call the course at which you intend to play and make sure they have club rentals (and shoes, too, if you intend to rent them). Let me be honest with you: It is a pain traveling with golf clubs, particularly if you are flying to your destination. At the same time, however, I really like playing with my own clubs. I can get away with using most rental clubs, but if I don't have my trusty putter with me I am lost. My rule of thumb is that if I'm going to play two rounds or more, I bring my clubs; if I'm only going to play one round, I don't.

I also never rent golf shoes. It's not that hard to put my golf shoes in my suitcase. I also bring my own golf gloves and a dozen golf balls to avoid paying a potential premium for buying them at the clubhouse. I also bring my little golf pouch with tees, a ball mark repair tool, and a ball marker.

How do you choose a golf course when you're not familiar with the area in which you are playing? My first step is to ascertain whether or not I know a local golfer who may be able to guide me to potential favorites. I tend to want to play on the best courses so long as it doesn't cost me as much as the airplane flight to get there.

If you belong to a club at home, your local golf pro can often arrange for you to play golf on a private course wherever you are traveling to. Even if your golf pro can't get you on another course, he may at least be able to provide you with a few recommendations of good clubs in the area.

If I have no inside knowledge of golf courses in the city I'm visiting, I typically go to the rankings established by *Golf Digest* or *Golf Magazine*. Although I may miss a gem because it's not publicized enough to get nationwide attention, it is better to play on a good quality course than to take any chances on an unknown quantity. It also never hurts to go on the Internet and see how other golfers rank different courses in the area.

Making a tee time at another golf course is not that different from making one in your home state. There are agencies that will handle scheduling this for you, or you can contact the pro shop directly. All the same rules apply when making a tee time at another destination: If you make a tee time and you end up not being able to play, have the courtesy to call the pro shop and cancel. It is highly likely the pro shop will require a credit card to hold the tee time (particularly because the pro shop knows you are coming from a distance and are not local), so make sure you know how far in advance you have to cancel the tee time to avoid being charged.

Often the pro shop will simply let you go out and play by yourself, particularly if it is a slow day. This is better than not playing at all, but I much prefer playing with a local golfer or filling in a threesome. It is very helpful playing with golfers who know the course, and it doesn't hurt to develop contacts in places you hope to visit again in the future.

I will caution you, however, that I do not think it is a great idea to play a match with people with whom you are not familiar. It is not because you may get ripped off for a lot of money, because golf matches are typically not highly staked. However, you do not know how your game compares to that of others and you do not know the disposition of your potential playing partner. Typically, I will simply tell the other players that I do not want to interfere with their usual game and I encourage them to play a match among the three of them. Having read the chapter on different kinds of informal group matches, you are in the perfect position to recommend the perfect game for a threesome. If you feel it necessary to "go along with the group" and play a match, suggest an individual match such as Wolf or Bingo Bango Bongo, thus avoiding disappointing an unknown partner. Whenever you feel comfortable joining a match, do so. Do not feel required or intimidated into playing a match if you don't want to. Just be upfront about it when you meet your group.

Remember you are obligated to post your score for handicap purposes. The GHIN system recognizes that you are playing on an unfamiliar course when you record it as an "away" game.

THE NINETEENTH HOLE

The nineteenth hole is the bar in the clubhouse. It is a place for your group to commiserate about your round, check your scores, see who won the match, and pay off your debts. One of the most ironic aspects of golf betting is that, typically, the team or player who wins the match pays for the first round of drinks. Don't ask me why. I never understood this. It seems to me that if the winner spends all of his winnings buying drinks, he would have been better off losing. Nonetheless, since I tend to lose more than I win, this works out just fine for me. But be a gracious loser: The winner should only have to pay for one round of drinks. A good loser will buy the second round or the bowl of nuts if you have sufficient time before heading out.

No one likes a bad loser. If you lose the match, do so in a sportsmanlike manner. Don't say it wasn't fair, don't whine about the uneven teams, and don't say you should've gotten more strokes. A good loser is invited back; a bad loser has to hunt for people to play with.

You may be lucky and get to the clubhouse right around the time a golfer hits a hole in one. If this is the case, it is customary for the golfer to buy a round of drinks for everyone in the clubhouse. In the event this happens to you (and congratulations if it does), this does not mean you have to buy drinks for everyone who walks in the clubhouse that entire day. Make sure you tell the golf pro that you hit a hole in one. Most courses will give you a little memento of the event. Also, if you happen to hit a hole in one, don't dismiss it as pure luck. That may be true, but savor the moment and take full credit for your fifteen minutes of fame.

TIPPING

Assuming you are playing on a course that allows tipping, be generous to the staff who work very hard to make your round pleasant. You certainly should tip the food server in the clubhouse just as if you were in a restaurant. Typically, when you drive your cart up to the clubhouse after your round, a "bag boy" (or man) will be waiting to take your clubs off the cart. He will typically wipe down your clubs and place them on the bag rack for your retrieval. Tip him. He deserves it. I usually tip $2.00 to $5.00 depending on the quality of the course and how good my round was (listen, I can't help it if a bad round makes me grumpy and less generous).

JOINING A CLUB

Should you join a golf club or play a variety of golf courses during your golf season? This, too, is a matter of personal preference. There are advantages to joining a club: You will be treated preferentially because, obviously, you are the financial backbone of the course. You will be able to play in a variety of course tournaments, leagues, and trophy competitions. If you play at one club all the time you get to learn all the nooks and crannies of the golf course and, presumably, you'll play better on your home course than away. A downside? You learn all the nooks and crannies of the golf course and, presumably, play better on your home course than away! That's right, you get a false sense of security because you have learned on what holes to lay up, when to hit to the right side of the course to avoid the left green-side bunker, when to be aggressive, and when to play it safe. Playing at a variety of courses teaches you how to play on a variety of courses!

In addition, every course has its own unique beauty and challenges. If you play a diverse range of courses, you see an array of fairways, roughs, green speeds, and hazards; you learn how to adapt to and handle different obstacles; and all this will help to instill flexibility in your game. At the end of the day it comes down to your personal preference, but if you do join a club I would still encourage you to play at some other courses periodically throughout the season to get a broader perspective on the big wide world of golf.

JOKES

Everyone likes a good joke. Obviously, I love a good joke, so I started each chapter with one to provide you with ample material to entertain your golfmates the next time you play golf. However, as is true about any other aspect of comedy, timing is everything.

Do not get to the first tee and start telling a joke. It's not the time because everyone is worrying about his or her first drive hitting a tree. Wait a little bit. Take your time. The perfect opportunity to tell a joke will arrive.

Be sensitive to the group with whom you're playing. If you are playing with a woman or a priest you may want to avoid an off-color joke ("A priest, minister, and rabbi walk into a pro shop together..."). This is not to suggest that women and priests don't have a sense of humor; it is to suggest that if you don't know your audience, err on the side of caution. If you know the right time to tell a joke at a party, it shouldn't be that difficult for you to use your common sense on the golf course.

The best time to tell a joke is when the group in front of you is just hitting their tee shot and you know you have plenty of time to start and finish your joke. Nothing is more irritating than starting a joke and not being able to finish it because a member of your group is about to tee off. However, if you haven't finished your joke by the time your group is supposed to tee off, do not delay the game by finishing your joke. Just time it better next time. Also, make sure your team is far enough away from the group on the tee so that when you tell your joke (which hopefully will result in an eruption of laughter) no one's concentration will be disturbed.

There are times that one of my playing partners is having such a terrible round that I tell him a joke just to take his mind off his game and lighten his mood. I save my shorter jokes for those situations.

And, of course, the nineteenth hole is an ideal time and place to tell a joke.

COLLECTING GOLF MEMORABILIA

Golf can be more than just trudging through eighteen holes and trying to figure out how you could play so well last week and forget everything you thought you knew during this round. If you are a collector, golf is a fertile field of memorabilia.

You can certainly buy pictures of your favorite golfer, or a flag from the Masters signed by that year's winner. But I find it's most fun to collect those items that are actually part of the game and not just designed to become a collectible.

I have a logo golf ball from every course I have played on. I am well into my second hundred and you can easily find very nice, yet reasonably priced, cases in which to put your logo balls.

I previously mentioned the desirability of having a tag identifying your ownership of your golf bag. Many courses have tags that identify you and the golf course, and these tags can be fun to collect.

I have golfing pals who collect a scorecard from every course they have played. Golf ball green markers and green mark repair tools from various courses can also bring back fond memories of your outings when snow is covering your favorite course. Whatever enhances your enjoyment of the game is a wonderful addition to your office or home.

SMOKING

I will get to cigars in a minute, but smokers typically find a golf course a safe haven to smoke cigarettes. Since I am a cigar smoker I will not judge cigarette smokers and suggest that they be banned from golf courses. However, a few basic rules of courtesy should apply. First, ask the individual in your cart if he minds you smoking. If he does, and if you have to smoke, make sure you do so out of the cart and when he's not around. Second, do not drop your cigarette butts haphazardly on the golf course. The course is heaven, not an ashtray. And third, dropping a lit cigarette in the woods in July may not bode well for the course, the local fire department, or your future.

CIGARS

Cigars and golf go together like hot dogs and mustard, like Laurel and Hardy, like chocolate and whipped cream. Each just makes the other better. Now this only applies to people who either like cigars, or do not hate people who like cigars. I admit that I love cigars. The only time I ever smoke a cigar is on the golf course. I would never think of smoking one in my house, my office, my car, or anywhere else on the planet. But, ahh, golf and cigars. They go together like Astaire and Rogers, like the Lone Ranger and Tonto, like. . .okay, now that I have lost total control of my senses, let me just say that the same basic etiquette for cigarette smoking applies to cigar smoking as well.

I always carry extra cigars with me in my golf bag. Playing golf with other people is a good way of making friends for life, and offering a cigar to partners during a round puts you in their Golf Hall of Fame. I also have a cutter and a lighter in my bag. Matches seldom work on a golf course, even if there's supposedly no wind blowing that day. It never fails that the one moment I try to light a cigar, Hurricane Hannah blows in from the west. Get a good lighter and carry it in your bag (but remember to take it out if you are traveling on an airplane with your golf clubs).

DRINKING

Listen, I'm all for drinking and some of my best friends are much more fun to be around if they've had a beer or two. However, excessive drinking and golf is as bad a combination as excessive drinking and driving (not to minimize the potential deadly consequences of drunk driving, of course). The point is that a completely normal golfer can become a very abusive golfer if alcohol combines with a duck hook. If you have as hard a time not drinking while playing golf as I do refraining from a cigar on the course, then by all means have a beer or two. Just know your limit and know the effect of alcohol on your demeanor and your golf swing. And needless to say, if your playing partner is drinking to excess, say to him exactly what you would say to him at a party: You've had too much to drink, you're becoming obnoxious, and give me the keys to the cart. And, while you're at it, don't let him drink in the bar after the round, and take his car keys away if he tries to drive home.

BEVERAGE AND FOOD CART

If you are lucky, the course on which you are playing will have a beverage and food cart. A couple of basic rules of courtesy to observe. First, the cart usually travels in the opposite direction of play. In other words, the cart will be coming from the green you are hitting toward. The experienced cart driver will see that you are hitting and will keep a safe distance away before approaching your group. When you see the cart approaching, ask everyone in the group if anyone is interested in something to eat or drink. If not, don't hesitate to wave the cart onward so the driver doesn't waste time stopping for your group.

It is not unusual for a member of the golf group to treat everyone else to a beverage or snack. Don't feel obligated to do so and don't hesitate to offer to reimburse someone who paid for you. And if someone else offers to buy you a beverage or snack, feel free to offer to pay the tip.

Tip the snack-cart driver. It is usually a female and she works very hard taking care of a variety of personalities that she encounters throughout the day. Tip her well and she will come around to your group more often. I tip a cart driver a minimum of $5.00 no matter how much we purchased from her, and if we buy a ton of stuff I tip her as I would a waitress.

Finally, the woman who drives the snack cart has heard every dirty joke and every pickup line you consider original and entertaining. And trust me when I tell you that they're neither original nor entertaining. Treat her as you would your daughter.

EATING

It is hard to play eighteen holes of golf without eating something during the round. A quick energy bar is fast and painless. If you bring or buy something more substantial, be conscious of not slowing down the game because your sandwich is falling all over your lap (a second use for your golf towel).

Some groups will stop in the clubhouse after the front nine to either buy a quick sandwich and then head out to the tenth tee, or to sit down and have lunch before heading out for the back nine. Keep in mind that if you stop for lunch, you give up your place and the groups behind you would gain priority when starting the back nine. Even if you are in the clubhouse just to pick up sandwiches to eat during the remainder of your round, if the group behind you is heading out to the tenth hole before you complete your transactions, that group has the right of way.

MOTHER NATURE

A woman golfer once described a golf course as "a man's urinal." This was said with complete jealousy. Now I'm not suggesting that you should go out of your way to "relieve" yourself in the local woods when you are looking for your ball. In fact, I don't know of any course that will say it's acceptable protocol to pee in the woods. But this is a book of practicality. And practicality dictates that there will be a time when those two beers are catching up to you and there is not a public restroom in sight. If (and once again I am NOT telling you that it is okay to pee on a golf course, wink wink) you have no choice but to use the woods as your urinal, be discreet, be well hidden, and make it quick (in other words don't slow down the game). Otherwise, have fun.

SAFETY

One of my very dear friends loved the game of golf. He was a good golfer and he and his wife often savored quality time as a couple playing golf with friends. One round, his playing partner hit a bad shot and instead of waiting for everyone else to hit his or her drive, he went out to the woods to look for his ball. He was not going to come back to the tee box, so my friend had to go ahead and hit his drive. As bad luck would have it, his drive struck his friend in the head. He passed out and it was later determined that he had suffered a concussion. He could have been killed. It was not my friend's fault, but he refused to ever play golf again. This deprived me of being able to play with him, and deprived him of enjoying the game in his twilight years.

The point is that unsafe golf can kill you. Stand a safe distance from someone preparing to hit. Stand a safe distance from him when he is taking his practice swing. Keep your eye on the hitter at all times and be aware of where his ball is going. Never walk in front, or to the blind side, of someone preparing to hit. Stay a very safe distance from anyone remotely preparing to hit a golf ball.

And if you are the hitter, be aware of everyone else in the group. Where are they standing, what are they doing, are they paying attention? Do not take a practice swing without knowing the location of every human being within ten feet of you. And if you have a bad shot, do not slam your club on the ground and do not fling your iron across the fairway. The ball or your club is a weapon that can hurt, maim, or kill. Treat it as you would a knife.

If you ever hurt someone while playing golf you will never feel good about playing the game again. Do not deprive yourself of this lifetime enjoyment and do not deprive someone else of his or her life.

A JOKE TO TELL YOU WHILE YOU'RE HAVING A BEER AFTER YOUR ROUND.

AFTER BEING STRANDED ON A DESERT ISLAND FOR TEN YEARS, WILSON SEES A SPECK ON THE HORIZON GROW CLOSER AND LARGER. FINALLY, AN INCREDIBLY BEAUTIFUL REDHEAD EMERGES FROM THE OCEAN IN A WET SUIT AND SCUBA GEAR.

"HEY, HANDSOME," DONNA GREETS HIM. "HOW LONG HAS IT BEEN SINCE YOU'VE HAD A CIGARETTE?"

"TEN YEARS," WILSON BARELY SPITS OUT. DONNA REACHES OVER, UNZIPS THE WATERPROOF POCKET ON HER SLEEVE, AND PULLS OUT A PACK OF FRESH CIGARETTES. WILSON LIGHTS ONE WITH TREMBLING HANDS.

DONNA THEN ASKS, "HOW LONG HAS IT BEEN SINCE YOU'VE HAD A SIP OF JAMESON IRISH WHISKEY?"

WILSON CAN BARELY CONTAIN HIS EXCITEMENT. "TEN YEARS," HE REPLIES. DONNA REACHES OVER TO THE POCKET ON HER OTHER SLEEVE AND PULLS OUT A FLASK. WILSON TAKES A LONG DRAW, WIPES HIS MOUTH, AND SAYS, "I CAN'T BELIEVE HOW SWEET THAT TASTES."

DONNA THEN SLOWLY BEGINS TO UNZIP THE ZIPPER ON THE FRONT OF HER WETSUIT. "AND HOW LONG HAS IT BEEN SINCE YOU'VE PLAYED AROUND?"

WILSON LOOKS AT DONNA WITH UNABASHED EXCITEMENT. "DON'T TELL ME YOU HAVE A SET OF GOLF CLUBS IN THERE?"

Chapter 18

The Last Putt: The Final Word on Golfing

LESSONS

You become a golfer by playing, learning, and practicing. There is no escaping the fact that golf does not come naturally to human beings. I have heard many a beginning golfer say that he or she is a "natural athlete" so this "game" will not be difficult for them to pick up. The next summer they are playing badminton.

How did I become a golfer? First, I took a series of individual lessons with an instructor certified by the PGA. However, finding the right teaching professional is as personal as finding the right playing partner: You learn best when you work together as a team. So feel free to try out different instructors. You can stick with one when he or she is clearly the "right one" for you, or just use a series of instructors. I have always learned something from every lesson I have ever taken.

A word of caution about sexism and female instructors. I have found that beginning women golfers feel more comfortable with a female instructor than a male instructor. I have decided that it is analogous to women always going to the bathroom in groups (and I have never figured out why they do this, although my therapist wife insists that it is a trade secret and she would have to kill me if I ever found out the reason). At the same time, I will tell you that some of the best golf lessons I have ever received were from female instructors. Men, don't reject taking a lesson from a woman out of ego or sexism. Women, don't rule out taking a lesson from a male instructor. A good instructor can teach a man or a woman.

I learned golf basics in my first series of lessons. Without a foundation to build upon, every swing that follows will reinforce bad habits that become harder to break the longer you play. However, I didn't take lessons every week for three years before hitting the links. I generally took six lessons in a row and then played two or three months without a lesson, repeating this pattern throughout my early golf-playing days. After I determined that my swing was generally set and it was unlikely that this leopard was going to change spots, I focused on one particular aspect of my game. I took a Dave Pelz putting lesson and a lesson in sand-trap play from my favorite Maine instructor, Paul Piveronis. After you get your basics down, taking a lesson that zeroes in on one part of your game will greatly improve your learning curve on that aspect of your swing.

Sometimes, when I travel, I may opt to take a lesson at a local club instead of playing golf. Because every golf instructor has a different style of play and emphasizes a different facet of the game, I find that drawing from a variety of pros around the country helps to give me a deeper understanding of how to play better. When I was in St. Augustine, after I played at TPC Sawgrass, I had a chipping lesson with golf professional Pomp Braswell. It was the best one-hour investment I have ever made.

GOLF SCHOOLS

I have attended a number of golf schools and I have loved every experience. However, I do not recommend attending a golf school until you are confident that you have learned the basics of golf. I do not believe a golf school is the place to learn how to play golf — it is the place to analyze and improve your game.

PRACTICE

No one really likes to practice. But I promise you that you will never get better at golf if you don't practice the game. So in between your rounds of golf, take an hour or so and head out to your local driving range. I always try to schedule an hour of practice in between each round of golf.

Some tips on how to make the most of your time on the range: Do not spend 90 percent of your time practicing your drive. Remember that you will use your driver fourteen times during a round of golf (presuming you will not use your driver on the four par 3s). You will hit your irons, wedges, and putter far more than your driver. Practice each club in proportion to how many times you'll use it during a round. If you spend half your time chipping and putting, a quarter of your time with irons, an eighth of your time with your fairway woods, and an eighth of your time with your driver, it will translate into a much better practice than banging out drives for an hour.

By the way, if you want the golfers around you and the caretakers of the range to think you know something about golf, make your range shots in a pattern so that the divots are contained in a small area. In other words, don't keep looking for a nice patch of green grass, far away from those awfully distracting divots, to hit your next shot. Go down a line as you hit so that your divots form a continuous furrow. Then start a second row. It looks cool, it shows you know what you are doing, and it is easier for the course to repair that part of the range for future practice.

Also, don't forget to spend a significant amount of time on the practice putting green. Remember the adage "drive for show, putt for dough." If you can keep your putting average to no more than two putts every green, your handicap will always remain under 20. If your facility has a

The golfer on the left practices like a pro; the amateur on the right wastes precious ground.

practice sand trap, use it regularly. Nothing helps you get out of a sand trap during a round better than having the confidence that comes with having practiced this shot twenty-five times a week.

PLAY

Just as you won't get better if you don't practice, you won't get better if you don't play golf. You also won't play well if you play golf once a month. What you'll get is frustrated and eventually you'll stop playing altogether.

Do not ignore the nine-hole round. Having a severe case of time urgency, I find it difficult to carve out the five hours necessary to play an eighteen-hole round on a frequent basis. But my playing partner and I can easily play a nine-hole round in under two hours. That fits our style perfectly, because it allows us to play at least once or twice a week, while maintaining a rigorous work schedule. I endeavor to play at least twice a week and practice at least an hour twice each week. I would prefer more, but unless I am incapacitated I never do less.

OFF-SEASON PLAY

If you live in a state in which inclement weather prevents you from playing year-round, do not put your clubs in the closet until spring. Find an indoor facility that allows you to practice and to keep your swing and body in shape. True, it is not as satisfying as playing a round of golf in the Florida sun, but one has to make do with what one has available. Most areas have an indoor golf simulator within reasonable driving distance. Although I do not find these simulators particularly similar to playing outside, my goal is not to score well on a machine, but to keep my muscles in shape and my swing embedded in my muscle memory. I practice indoors once a week if I am unable to play in Maine or at a winter retreat.

PHYSICAL CONDITIONING

The off-season is also an ideal time to improve your physical stamina and condition. Since I play lots of golf during my free time during the warm weather months, I focus on exercise during the winter months (which, in Maine, is every day except July 4th). Doing the treadmill on a regular basis during my off months allows me to walk eighteen holes my first time out in spring. Winter is also a terrific time to experiment with non-traditional golf conditioning: Take a yoga or meditation class. Although they're not standard golf preparation, you may find both contribute to the improvement of your game when the spring season begins.

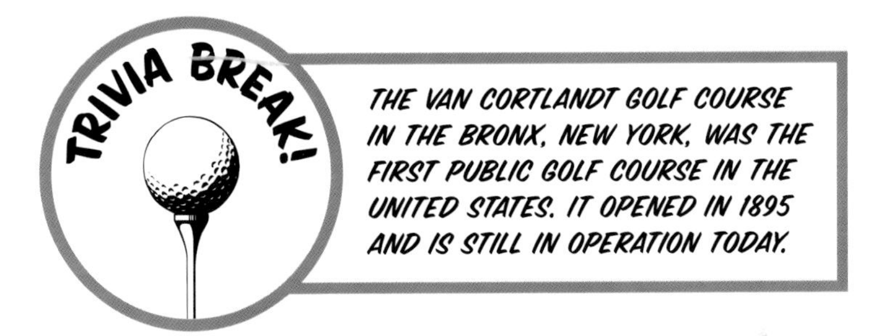

HAVE FUN

A final reminder that golf is a game and games are supposed to be fun. If you are not having fun playing golf, it defeats the whole purpose of the game. Go out, meet people, compete with others, compete with yourself, or just take a nice walk on the velvety carpet of the fairway. Be thankful you are alive and you can enjoy the respite from the rigors of everyday life that golf affords you. And make sure that next time you come to my town you give me a call. I'll meet you on the first tee at a quarter past the hour.

Acknowledgments

First and foremost, I must give my profound thanks to my wife of twenty-nine years, Lynda Doyle. Not only did she give me my first set of golf clubs (Calloway X-12s), but she showed me how I could channel my ADHD in such a way that I could write a book while practicing law full-time and hosting a morning radio show.

My oldest daughter Amy, who tried to play golf (but wasn't crazy about it), and gives me a beautiful Bobby Jones golf shirt every Christmas.

My youngest daughter, Chelsea, who also tried to play (and also wasn't crazy about it), and edited this book. She is a better writer than me and should have written a book before me.

My father, Jerome, who played golf twice a week during my youth. In those days, fathers played with their buddies more than their children, but I always envied his respite from work. It took me until I was forty-five to take up the game, but better late than never. And my father and I have had some wonderful outings ever since.

My brothers, Larry and Mike, who play on occasion, but can't stand their little brother beating them at any game. They should stick with tennis.

I am proud to belong to the American Academy of Matrimonial Lawyers, a national organization of 1,650 lawyers specializing in family law. In 2003, our then President, Richard Barry, asked me to be the director of our annual March golf tournament. I have continued to be honored with this assignment ever since. I should note that another past president, Gary Nickelson, from Dallas, Texas, named the trophy awarded annually to the winning team the "Eat, Drink, and Remarry Trophy" (and he took me to play at the Colonial in Ft. Worth last year).

A special thanks to my golfing friends who reviewed, edited, and critiqued my manuscript: Rob Baldacci, Jim McLaren, Ken Bailey, and my soon to be son-in-law, Preston Noon, who will play with me even though my daughter will not. And not to forget my secretary, Beth Webster, who always managed to book time for me to play golf whenever I got too cranky.

A special thanks to my publisher, Ronnie Sellers, and his son, Lindsey, who inspired me to write this book the first time I played golf with them and realized they had no clue as to the rules of golf. Also, a special thanks to my editor, Mark Chimsky-Lustig, who doesn't play golf, but if golf editors had handicaps he would be a scratch editor. And thanks as well to Charlotte Cromwell, Sellers' assistant production editor, who did such a great job putting the pages of this book together coherently, to proofreader *par excellence* Bob Holtzman, and to Steve Dinberg, whose photographs so perfectly capture the beauty of this game. A huge thank you to Leslie Evans, truly one of the most gifted designers I have ever known, for not only art directing and styling the cover of the book, but encouraging my effort throughout the process. And to François Gagné who took the wonderful photograph on the front cover that caught your attention. A thank you to my attorneys, Kenneth Weinrib, Jake Levy, and Eric Brown, who may not know how to play golf, but certainly know everything about contracts for writers of golf books.

Another special thanks to my dear friends, Rodney "Chip" Gray and Christiane Northrup. Chip is part owner of the Harraseeket Inn in Freeport, Maine, where I spent many an hour drafting and rewriting this book by the fireplace in the Tavern. Chris is one of the most progressive and innovative doctors of our generation and you should watch every one of her PBS specials and read every one of her books. You probably already have. Both Chip and Chris encouraged me relentlessly.

I cannot name all of the individuals with whom I have played golf over the years, but I will try to recount the most memorable of the lot: My favorite golf partner on a regular basis is Rob Baldacci, who plays every time I call and will even turn off his cell phone if I beg him to do so. Rob, thanks for being a great golfing partner. His brother, John, the best governor the State of Maine has ever had, would be equally my favorite partner if he didn't waste so much of his time working on something he calls "the State budget." I am very much looking forward to the day he retires from civil service so I can play with him weekly.

My teammates and favorite golf partners during the annual AAML tournament: Jim McLaren, Pat McLaren, and Bob Moses. Three other golfing lawyers who frequent the links with me during the AAML meetings: Walter Lesnevich, Dan Hoffnung, and Fred Harwell. Mark Russell is the oldest friend I have who still talks to me. I didn't play golf when we met, but we both do now. And he donated some of the best jokes to this book. Mike Violette, my co-host on our morning radio show (560 WGAN, Portland, Maine), who too often covered for me while I was editing this book (and who often plays golf with me when we recover from our political debates). My program director, Jeff Wade, who didn't say anything when I was editing this book between segments of our show, and my producer, Andrew Baker, who didn't tell

Jeff I was editing this book during segments. And the man who hired me for the radio show (telling me I could quit if I didn't like it after a month or two — seven years ago) — Cary Pahigian.

The other notable golfers with whom I have played — and I must have enjoyed it because I remember them now: Dana Cleaves, Bill Nugent, Kevin Heikkinen, Mike Malcolm, Rick DeFilipp, Seth Goodall, LeAnn Greenleaf, and John McElwee. Thanks for being a major part of my golf life.

My good friend (and, needless to say, a better lawyer and writer), F. Lee Bailey, who guided me throughout this writing process (with the support of his dear significant other, Debbie Elliott). And, finally, my law partner, Derry Rundlett, who has the best and most positive attitude about golf of anyone I have ever met. And his wife, Marilyn, who encourages Derry to be Derry.

A thanks to Dick Harris, who has virtually single-handedly made golf a staple of Maine life. Many thanks to the staff at my home club, The Woodlands in Falmouth, Maine, with a particular nod to Head Pro Doug Van Wickler, Assistant Pro John Mullen, Pro Tony Decker, and the remaining crew in and out of the pro shop who never fail to get me to the first tee on time, every time. Also, Andy Richardson who always has a Stella waiting when I get off the eighteenth green, and the wait staff, who tolerate every story I tell about that chip-in I made for par on the fifth hole. And, finally, to the many professionals who have contributed to my learning (and enjoyment) of the game, particularly my number-one teacher, Paul Piveronis.

Author Bio

photo © Lynda Doyle

KEN ALTSHULER hails from Oklahoma City, Oklahoma, and currently resides with his wife, Dr. Lynda Doyle, two bichons and one Boston terrier, in Durham, Maine (by way of the University of Michigan). His two daughters, Amy and Chelsea, live in Manhattan, where there are some very good golf stores, but very few golf courses.

Besides thinking, eating, and sleeping golf, Ken has been practicing law in Portland since 1985, where he is a partner at Childs, Rundlett, Fifield & Altshuler. Ken's practice focuses exclusively on Family Law. He is a member of the American College of Family Trial Lawyers and the International Academy of Matrimonial Lawyers. He is also a Fellow and the President Elect of the American Academy of Matrimonial Lawyers. Ken is included in the exclusive *Best Lawyers in America* and is distinguished as a Lawdragon Finalist and a New England Super Lawyer.

Ken is the co-host for Portland, Maine's number-one morning radio talk show, the WGAN "Morning News with Ken and Mike." Finally, and most significantly, he currently has a 17.3 handicap index.